Benghazi Attacks: Investigative Update
Interim Report on the Accountability Review Board

Staff Report Prepared for Chairman Darrell Issa
U.S. House of Representatives
113th Congress
Committee on Oversight and Government Reform

September 16, 2013

Contents

Table of Names

> Department of State

Eric Boswell
Assistant Secretary for Diplomatic Security

Eric Boswell is the former Assistant Secretary for Diplomatic Security. He was one of four State Department employees named by the ARB. Boswell resigned his position as Assistant Secretary for Diplomatic Security, but Under Secretary for Management Ambassador Patrick Kennedy asked him to remain in his concurrent position as the Director of the Office of Foreign Missions. Boswell was placed on administrative leave in December 2012, immediately after the ARB released its report.

Scott Bultrowicz
Director, Diplomatic Security Service

Scott Bultrowicz is the former Director of the Diplomatic Security Service. He was Eric Boswell's deputy at the Bureau of Diplomatic Security. Bultrowicz was placed on administrative leave on December 2012.

Elizabeth Dibble
Principal Deputy Assistant Secretary, Bureau of Near Eastern Affairs

Elizabeth Dibble is the Principal Deputy Assistant Secretary for Near Eastern Affairs. She is Elizabeth Jones' deputy, and the second most senior official in the Bureau of Near Eastern Affairs.

Jeffrey Feltman
Assistant Secretary, Bureau of Near Eastern Affairs

Jeffrey Feltman was the Assistant Secretary for the Bureau of Near Eastern Affairs from August 18, 2009 until May 31, 2012. In December 2011, Feltman requested that Under Secretary for Management Patrick Kennedy approve a continued *ad hoc* U.S. presence in Benghazi through the end of calendar year 2012. Kennedy approved.

Gregory Hicks
Deputy Chief of Mission, Libya

Gregory Hicks is the former Deputy Chief of Mission in Libya. He testified before the Committee on May 8, 2013, describing in detail the events on the ground and his interactions with Ambassador Chris Stevens on September 11, 2012. The State Department assigned him to a desk job while he awaits an onward assignment.

Elizabeth Jones
Acting Assistant Secretary, Bureau of Near Eastern Affairs

Elizabeth Jones is the Acting Assistant Secretary for Near Eastern Affairs, the most senior official in the Bureau of Near Eastern Affairs. Jones was the direct supervisor of Raymond Maxwell, the former Deputy Assistant Secretary for Maghreb Affairs.

Patrick F. Kennedy
Under Secretary of State for Management

Patrick Kennedy, a Career Minister in the Foreign Service, has served as the Under Secretary of State since 2007. Kennedy approved a memorandum that requested to continue the *ad hoc* U.S. presence in Benghazi through the end of calendar year 2012.

Charlene Lamb
Deputy Assistant Secretary for International Programs

The ARB cited Charlene Lamb for failing to provide the requested number of diplomatic security agents at the Benghazi mission and ignoring efforts by her subordinates to improve the staffing challenges at the mission. Lamb was placed on administrative leave in December 2012.

Lee Lohman
Executive Director, Bureau of Near Eastern Affairs

Lee Lohman was the Executive Director of the Bureau of Near Eastern Affairs. Lohman testified that Raymond Maxwell was not involved in any decisions pertaining to the security at Benghazi, and that Patrick Kennedy was highly involved with security decisions that affected Benghazi.

Raymond Maxwell
Deputy Assistant Secretary for Maghreb Affairs

Raymond Maxwell was the only individual in the Bureau of Near Eastern Affairs with whom the ARB found fault for the Benghazi attacks. Several witnesses testified that both the ARB and the State Department treated Maxwell unfairly. Maxwell was placed on administrative leave in December 2012.

Brian Papanu
Desk Officer, Libya

Brian Papanu served as the Desk Officer for Libya. He was responsible for obtaining temporary duty staff for Libya and served as a liaison between Washington, D.C. and Tripoli.

William Roebuck
Director, Office of Maghreb Affairs

William Roebuck is the Deputy Assistant Secretary for Maghreb Affairs—the position previously held by Raymond Maxwell. He served as the Chargé d'Affaires to Libya from January to June 2013. Prior to that post, he served as the Director of the Office of Maghreb Affairs, where he was one of the most knowledgeable policymakers on Libya in the State Department. Roebuck considered shutting down the Benghazi mission due to lack of security.

➢ Accountability Review Board

Thomas R. Pickering
Chairman

During his distinguished career, Thomas Pickering served as U.S. Ambassador to Jordan, Nigeria, El Salvador, Israel, India, Russia, and the United Nations. Pickering has also served as Under Secretary for Political Affairs, the State Department's fourth-highest ranking official.

Michael G. Mullen
Vice Chairman

Michael Mullen is a retired four-star Navy admiral who served two terms as the Chairman of the Joint Chiefs of Staff, the highest ranking officer in the U.S. Armed Forces.

Catherine A. Bertini

Catherine Bertini is a former Executive Director of the United Nations World Food Programme. She later served as former Assistant Secretary of Food and Consumer Services at the U.S. Department of Agriculture. She is currently on the faculty at Syracuse University.

Richard J. Shinnick

During his long career with the Foreign Service, Richard Shinnick served as the Director for the Bureau of Overseas Buildings and Operations, Executive Director of the Bureau of Near Eastern and South Asian Affairs, and Executive Director of the Executive Secretariat. Shinnick has extensive experience in the Under Secretariat for Management.

Hugh J. Turner III

Hugh Turner is a former senior Intelligence Community official, and served as the Deputy Director of Operations for the Central Intelligence Agency.

Glossary

ARB – Accountability Review Board

DNI – Director of National Intelligence

DOD – Department of Defense

DS – Bureau of Diplomatic Security, U.S. Department of State

DSS – Diplomatic Security Service, Bureau of Diplomatic Security, U.S. Department of State

DS/IP – Bureau of Diplomatic Security, International Programs Office, U.S. Department of State

HFAC – U.S. House of Representatives, Committee on Foreign Affairs

IED – Improvised Explosive Device

LES – Locally Employed Staff

M/PRI – Office of Management Policy, Rightsizing and Innovation, U.S. Department of State

MSG – Marine Security Guard

NEA –Bureau of Near Eastern Affairs, U.S. Department of State

NSS – National Security Staff

OSPB – Overseas Security Policy Board

RSO – Regional Security Officer

SECCA – Secure Embassy Construction and Counterterrorism Act of 1999

SST – Security Support Team

TDY – Temporary Duty Assignment

Benghazi Accountability Review Board: Key Concerns

- The structure of the ARB and culture within the State Department raised questions about the independence and integrity of the review.

- The ARB blamed systemic failures and leadership and management deficiencies within two bureaus, but downplayed the importance of decisions made at senior levels of the Department. Witnesses questioned how much these decisions influenced the weaknesses that led to the inadequate security posture in Benghazi.

- Witnesses questioned whether the ARB went far enough in considering the challenges of expeditionary diplomacy.

- The ARB's decision to cite certain officials as accountable for what happened in Benghazi appears to have been based on factors that had little or no connection to the security posture at U.S. diplomatic facilities in Libya.

- The haphazard decision to place the four officials cited by the ARB on paid administrative leave created the appearance that former Secretary Hillary Clinton's decision to announce action against the individuals named in the ARB report was more of a public relations strategy than a measured response to a tragedy.

Benghazi Accountability Review Board: Unanswered Questions

- What specific documentary evidence and witness testimony did the ARB review to reach its conclusions?

- What changes are necessary to eliminate the real or perceived lack of independence in the ARB structure?

- Did Secretary Clinton have views on the need to extend the Benghazi mission, both in the fall of 2011 and summer of 2012? Was she consulted on these questions and what, if any, influence did her opinion have on the Department's decisions?

- Is the State Department resistant to elevating the importance of security considerations?

- Why did the State Department fail to establish an Under Secretary for Security, as recommended by an external review and approved by Secretary of State Madeleine Albright, following the attacks in East Africa in 1998?

- Why did the Best Practices Panel strongly recommend that the State Department establish an Under Secretary for Security? Why did the Benghazi ARB not recommend such a change?

- Why did it take the State Department eight months to evaluate the performance of the four individuals placed on administrative leave? What information did Secretary Kerry and his staff review as part of that process? Who was involved in the process?

- How much did the decision to extend the Benghazi mission as a temporary facility limit the Department's ability to provide security resources?

- Who should be held accountable for deciding to extend the Benghazi mission as a temporary facility?

Executive Summary

The September 11, 2012 terrorist attacks on the U.S. diplomatic facilities in Benghazi, Libya resulted in a tragic and unnecessary loss of American life. The attacks also raise a number of important and substantive questions about U.S. foreign policy, with which policymakers will have to grapple for some time. A key area for further discussion and analysis is the balance between the U.S. Department of State's policy imperative of operating diplomatic outposts abroad and the security realities of doing so in dangerous and unstable environments such as Libya.

Pursuant to statutory requirement under the Omnibus Diplomatic Security and Terrorism Act of 1986, Secretary of State Hillary Clinton convened an Accountability Review Board (ARB) shortly after the attacks to address these questions. The five-member Board comprised distinguished public servants, including Chairman Thomas Pickering, former U.S. Ambassador to six countries and the United Nations, and Vice Chairman Michael Mullen, former Chairman of the Joint Chiefs of Staff.

The ARB operated under significant time pressure, completing its work and issuing a final report in just over two months. The State Department widely supported the ARB's recommendations, and sought to implement them without hesitation. For some, including the Department itself, this report represented the final word on the internal failures that contributed to the tragedy in Benghazi. For others, however, the report overvalued certain facts, overlooked others, and failed to address systemic issues that have long plagued the State Department.

In order to address these concerns, the Committee held a hearing on May 8, 2013, entitled, "Benghazi: Exposing Failure and Recognizing Courage." Not only did the testimony of three State Department officials—Mark Thompson, Eric Nordstrom, and Gregory Hicks— provide important information to Committee Members about the fateful attacks, it raised additional questions about the attacks as well as the ARB's work. In light of these questions, the Committee initiated a comprehensive investigation of the ARB procedures, findings, and recommendations. Understanding how the ARB reached its conclusions informs the Committee's interest in ensuring that this process remains efficient and effective, and that U.S. diplomats are able to avoid situations that compromise their safety or their mission. This effort supplements and informs the Committee's ongoing, independent evaluation of the facts and circumstances of what transpired before, during, and after the attacks on Benghazi.

Since the May 8 hearing, the Committee has taken a number of steps to advance the Benghazi investigation. During that time, the Committee has obtained testimony from more than a dozen witnesses, conducting more than 50 hours of transcribed interviews. The Committee has requested additional interviews, including of survivors of the attacks. The Department has thus far declined to make these individuals available, despite the fact that these individuals were made available to the ARB and media outlets. Committee investigators have reviewed more than 25,000 pages of documents. The Department continues to identify new material responsive to numerous requests from the Committee. The Department's failure to produce responsive materials has left the Committee with no alternative but to issue subpoenas. Overall, despite many Committee attempts at accommodation, the State Department has been exceedingly uncooperative with the Committee's investigation of the attacks on Benghazi. Still, the Committee has been able to learn a great deal about the ARB's work.

While identifying positive and productive aspects of the ARB's review, witnesses interviewed by the Committee raised a number of significant concerns with the ARB process, findings, and recommendations. Most notably, several witnesses questioned the ARB's findings regarding the four Department employees held "accountable" for Benghazi. In some cases the ARB appeared to hold individuals accountable for actions which had nothing to do with security in Benghazi. In other cases, the ARB correctly identified poor individual decisions while apparently failing to take into account decisions made by more senior Department officials. Such senior-level decisions played an equal if not greater role in the vulnerability of the U.S. diplomatic mission in Benghazi. In particular, the ARB did not adequately address the decision by Department leadership to operate the Benghazi mission as a temporary and particularly ill-defended outpost of what it calls "expeditionary diplomacy." Nor did the ARB hold any individuals accountable for that decision.

The State Department's response to the ARB's findings on accountability is equally troubling. Secretary Clinton immediately relieved the four employees identified by the ARB of their duties and subsequently placed them on administrative leave – an ambiguous status akin to bureaucratic limbo. The Department misled these employees about what administrative leave entailed, did not allow the employees to challenge this decision, and further prohibited them access to the classified ARB Report, which contained the evidence against them. Moreover, the ARB failed to question these employees on the very topics for which they were held accountable. Last month, after eight months of paid administrative leave, Secretary of State John Kerry reinstated these four employees to Department service. Therefore, one year after the Benghazi attacks, no one at the State Department has been fired for their role leading up to the Benghazi attacks. It appears increasingly likely the Department's primary objective was to create the public appearance of accountability.

In addition, witnesses questioned whether the ARB properly addressed the challenges of increasing reliance on "expeditionary diplomacy." Some witnesses and stakeholders suggested that the ARB's recommendations improve on past failures but do not go far enough in striking the right balance between policy objectives and security realities. While the U.S. cannot advance its national interests from concrete bunkers and there is no such thing as 100 percent security, the highest levels of the Department must establish a clear line of responsibility for balancing foreign policy objectives with diplomatic security. One of the ARB's recommendations was that the State Department convene an independent best practices panel, comprised of security experts. The Panel identified a number of areas for improvement that the ARB did not address.

This interim report focuses exclusively on the ARB and its shortcomings. While the Committee presents current observations about the ARB gleaned through its investigation, it has also identified areas for further inquiry. Indeed, many serious questions surrounding Benghazi have gone unanswered. The Committee will continue its investigation wherever the facts lead.

Background

On September 11, 2012—now more than one year ago—armed extremists attacked a U.S. diplomatic facility in Benghazi, Libya. During these major attacks, terrorists overwhelmed the facility's guards and set fire to structures within the compound before diplomatic personnel inside could escape or reinforcements arrived. Four U.S. personnel were killed: Ambassador Christopher Stevens; State Department Information Officer Sean Smith; and two American security officers—and former U.S. Navy SEALs—Tyrone Woods and Glen Doherty.

On October 3, 2012, then-Secretary of State Hillary Rodham Clinton announced that the U.S. Department of State would convene an Accountability Review Board (ARB, or Board) to "examine the facts and circumstances of the attacks and to report findings and recommendations as it deems appropriate."[1] In addition, the Board was responsible for determining whether a "breach of duty" by any federal employee contributed to the attacks in Benghazi.

Approximately ten weeks later, on December 18, 2012, Secretary Clinton delivered the ARB Report to Congress.[2] Among other findings, the ARB concluded that "systemic failures and leadership and management deficiencies at senior levels within two bureaus" were to blame for the "inadequate" security posture at the U.S. facilities in Benghazi.[3]

The Administration has used this congressionally-mandated report to deflect questions about what transpired in Benghazi. Until the report was issued, Secretary Clinton and other Obama Administration officials regularly refused to answer questions about what happened in Benghazi, citing the ongoing ARB review. After the ARB Report was issued in December, Clinton and other top officials routinely referred questioners to the conclusions of the ARB Report. The White House and the State Department pointed to the ARB and its Report as the definitive final word on the failures that led to the attacks in Benghazi. White House Press Secretary Jay Carney stated:

> The Accountability Review Board which investigated this matter—and I think in no one's estimation sugarcoated what happened there or pulled any punches when it came to holding accountable individuals that they felt had not successfully executed their responsibilities—heard from everyone and invited everyone. So there was a clear indication there that everyone who had something to say was welcome to provide information to the Accountability Review Board.[4]

---

[1] Fed. Reg., Vol. 77, No. 193 (Oct. 4, 2012), at 60741, Pub. Notice 8052.

[2] Letter from Hon. Hillary R. Clinton, Sec'y, U.S. Dep't of State, to Hon. John F. Kerry, Chairman, Comm. on Foreign Relations, U.S. Senate (Dec. 18, 2012).

[3] Accountability Review Board, U.S. Dep't of State, Report (Dec. 18, 2012), *available at* http://www.state.gov/documents/organization/202446.pdf [hereinafter ARB Report].

[4] The White House, Office of the Press Sec'y, Press Briefing by Press Sec'y Jay Carney (May 1, 2013), http://www.whitehouse.gov/the-press-office/2013/05/01/press-briefing-press-secretary-jay-carney-512013.

State Department spokesman Patrick Ventrell further stated, "We think that we've done an independent investigation, that it's been transparent, thorough, credible, and detailed, and . . . we've shared those findings with the U.S. Congress."[5]

Months later, President Obama held up the work of the ARB as the symbol of the Administration's effort to identify the problems that led to the inadequate security posture in Benghazi. In response to a question about Benghazi at a May 13, 2013 press conference, the President said:

> The day after it happened, I acknowledged that this was an act of terrorism, and what I pledged to the American people is we would find out what happened, we would make sure that it did not happen again, and we would make sure we held accountable those who perpetrated this terrible crime. That's exactly what we've been trying to do. Over the last several months, there was a review board headed by two distinguished Americans – Mike Mullen and Tom Pickering – who investigated every element of this.[6]

Although the ARB made several findings that are consistent with facts uncovered by congressional investigators, the Committee's investigation has revealed that ARB did not go far enough in addressing systemic weaknesses within the State Department. In addition, while there is no question that the real accountability rests with the terrorists who carried out these heinous acts, the evidence the Committee has uncovered to date suggests that some of the ARB's findings related to accountability within the State Department were flawed.

Secretary Clinton was required by law to convene an Accountability Review Board.

Secretary Clinton convened the ARB pursuant to the Omnibus Diplomatic Security and Antiterrorism Act of 1986 (the Act), which states that "in any case of serious injury, loss of life, or significant destruction of property at, or related to, a United States Government mission abroad . . . the Secretary of State shall convene an Accountability Review Board."[7] The Benghazi ARB was the nineteenth Accountability Review Board held since 1988.[8]

---

[5] James Rosen, *State Department's Benghazi review panel under investigation*, FOXNEWS, May 2, 2013, http://www.foxnews.com/politics/2013/05/02/state-department-benghazi-review-panel-under-investigation-fox-news-confirms/#ixzz2ebmbG4yW.

[6] Remarks of President Barack Obama at a joint press conference with Prime Minister David Cameron (May 13, 2013).

[7] Omnibus Diplomatic Security and Antiterrorism Act of 1986, 22 U.S.C. § 4831(a)(1).

[8] Sec'y of State Hillary Rodham Clinton, Test. Before S. Comm. on Foreign Relations (Jan. 23, 2013), *available at* http://www.foreign.senate.gov/imo/media/doc/SECRETARY%20OF%20STATE%20HILLARY%20RODHAM%20CLINTON.pdf.

According to State Department regulations, the ARB has several functions and characteristics. First, it is intended to be **"thorough and independent."**[9] Second, it is intended to **"foster more effective security of U.S. missions and personnel abroad."**[10] Third, it is to **"determine accountability."**[11] Finally, it is to **"promote and encourage improved security programs and practices."**[12]

Under the statute, the Secretary must convene an ARB within 60 days of a security incident.[13] In deciding whether to convene an ARB, the Secretary relies on the ARB Permanent Coordinating Committee, a standing committee consisting of State Department officials in the management, diplomatic security, intelligence, counterterrorism, and political affairs bureaus and offices, as well as a representative of the Director of National Intelligence.[14] In addition, a permanent ARB staff officer serves as the "institutional memory" within the Department for all ARB-related matters and keeps a list of individuals qualified to be named to an ARB in the event that the Secretary must convene one.[15]

When the Secretary convenes an ARB, an Executive Secretary appointed by the Director of the Office of Management Policy, Rightsizing and Innovation (M/PRI), an office under the Under Secretary of State for Management, joins the staff. The ARB may also determine that it requires the Department to furnish additional experts and support staff to carry out its duties.[16]

Senior State Department officials appointed distinguished public servants to serve on the Benghazi ARB.

The Accountability Review Board that Secretary Clinton and Lieutenant General James R. Clapper, the Director of National Intelligence (DNI), assembled represented a high standard of professional achievement and dedication to public service. The Chairman of the ARB, Ambassador Thomas R. Pickering has served as the U.S. Ambassador to Jordan, Nigeria, El Salvador, Israel, the United Nations, India, and Russia. Pickering also served as the 17th Under Secretary for Political Affairs during President Bill Clinton's second term. The Vice Chairman, Admiral Michael G. Mullen, brought to the ARB over four decades of experience in the U.S. Navy, culminating in two terms as Chairman of the Joint Chiefs of Staff from 2007 to 2011. The other members of the Board were: Catherine Bertini, a professor with experience in foreign assistance in the private sector and with the United Nations; Richard J. Shinnick, a veteran Foreign Service officer with extensive experience in the Under Secretariat for Management; and Hugh J. Turner III, a former senior Intelligence Community official. Of the five ARB members,

---

[9] U.S. Dep't of State, Foreign Affairs Manual (FAM), Vol. 12, Diplomatic Security, 12 FAM 031.1 (emphasis added).
[10] *Id.* (emphasis added).
[11] *Id.* (emphasis added).
[12] *Id.* (emphasis added).
[13] 22 U.S.C. § 4831(b)(1). The statute also provides for a 60-day extension if needed. *Id.*
[14] 12 FAM 032.
[15] *Id.*; *see also* 12 FAM 033.
[16] 12 FAM 032.3

the Secretary of State selected four. DNI Clapper nominated the fifth, Hugh Turner, to serve on the ARB.[17]

As set forth by Secretary Clinton, the Benghazi ARB's specific mandate was to "determine whether our security systems and procedures in Benghazi were appropriate in light of the threat environment, whether those systems and procedures were properly implemented, and any lessons that may be relevant to our work around the world."[18] Announcing the ARB's creation, Secretary Clinton remarked, "The men and women who serve this country as diplomats deserve no less than **a full and accurate accounting wherever that leads**, and I am committed to seeking that for them."[19]

The Benghazi ARB worked under tight time constraints. It completed its work in approximately 10 weeks.

The Benghazi ARB first met in early October 2012. A principal source of information for the ARB was a series of interviews with key individuals, sometimes in a group setting, but more often individually.[20] Interviews Admiral Mullen described as "substantive" in nature lasted between two to four hours, while other interviews lasted about an hour.[21] While all ARB members were present for most interviews, this was not universally the case.[22] The ARB did not transcribe its interviews; rather reports indicate that ARB staff members took handwritten notes.[23] The State Department represented to the Committee that the ARB had access to approximately 7,000 documents numbering thousands of pages.[24] Ultimately, the unclassified report delivered to Congress on December 18, 2012 contained five findings and 24 recommendations.[25]

Upon delivery of the report, Secretary Clinton informed Congress of her intention to accept all of the Board's recommendations. In a letter to the relevant Committees of jurisdiction, the Secretary stated:

> I asked the Deputy Secretary for Management and Resources to lead a task force at the State Department to ensure that the Board's recommendations are implemented quickly and completely, as well as to pursue steps above and beyond those recommended in the Board's report. This group has already begun meeting, and the Deputy Secretary, along with the Undersecretary for Political Affairs, the Undersecretary for Management,

---

[17] Transcribed Interview of Adm. Michael G. Mullen (Ret.), Tr. at 18-19, (June 19, 2013) [hereinafter Mullen Tr.].
[18] Secretary Hillary Rodham Clinton, Remarks with Foreign Minister of Kazakhstan Erlan Idrissov After Their Meeting (Oct. 3, 2012), *available at* http://www.state.gov/secretary/rm/2012/10/198635 htm.
[19] *Id.* (emphasis added).
[20] Mullen Tr. at 22.
[21] Mullen Tr. at 30.
[22] Deposition of Amb. Thomas Pickering, Transcript at 13 (June 4, 2013) [hereinafter Pickering Tr.].
[23] Mullen Tr. at 29-30.
[24] Letter from Thomas B. Gibbons, Acting Ass't Sec., Leg. Affairs, U.S. Dep't of State, to Hon. Darrell E. Issa, Chairman, H. Comm. on Oversight & Gov't Reform (Aug. 23, 2013).
[25] In comparison, the classified report contained 29 total recommendations.

the Director General of the Foreign Service, and the Deputy Legal Advisor are driving this effort forward.

Because of steps we began taking in the hours and days after the attacks, this work is well underway. We will have implementation of every recommendation underway by the time the next Secretary of State takes office. There is no higher priority for me or my Department.[26]

On May 20, 2013, the State Department announced its progress on implementing each of the 24 unclassified ARB recommendations (see Appendix).

The ARB assigned accountability to four mid-level officials.

In addition to the recommendations on policy and procedures, the Benghazi ARB made personnel findings with regard to four State Department officials. The Board determined that none of these individuals breached their duties, as defined by the statute, and therefore could not be "the subject of a recommendation for disciplinary action."[27] The Board did, however, take the unprecedented step of including a specific finding regarding the performance of these four State Department officials, as well as recommendations for administrative actions against two of the individuals. In the unclassified report, the Board stated:

[C]ertain senior State Department officials within two bureaus in critical positions of authority and responsibility in Washington demonstrated a lack of proactive leadership and management ability appropriate for the Department's senior ranks in their responses to security concerns posed by Special Mission Benghazi, given the deteriorating threat environment and lack of reliable host government protection.[28]

The details of the Board's findings regarding these four individuals were reserved for the classified version of the report. On December 19, 2012, however, the identities of these individuals appeared in public media reports after the State Department announced that they had been "placed on administrative leave pending further action."[29]

Three of these officials served in the Bureau of Diplomatic Security, a component of the Under Secretariat for Management headed by Ambassador Patrick Kennedy. These officials were the Assistant Secretary of the Bureau of Diplomatic Security (DS), Eric Boswell, his deputy Scott Bultrowicz, and Deputy Assistant Secretary for International Programs Charlene Lamb. The fourth official, Raymond Maxwell, had been the Deputy Assistant Secretary for Maghreb

---

[26] Letter from Hon. Hillary Clinton, Sec'y, U.S. Dep't of State, to Hon. John F. Kerry, Chairman, S. Comm. on Foreign Affairs, et al. (Dec. 18, 2012) *available at* http://www.state.gov/documents/organization/202447.pdf.
[27] ARB Report at 39.
[28] *Id.*
[29] Michael R. Gordon & Eric Schmitt, *4 Are Out at State Dept. After Scathing Report on Benghazi Attack*, N.Y. TIMES, Dec. 19, 2012, http://www.nytimes.com/2012/12/20/us/politics/3-state-dept-officials-resign-following-benghazi-report.html?_r=0.

Affairs and was the only individual in the Bureau of Near Eastern Affairs – a component of the Under Secretariat of Political Affairs – to whom the ARB assigned blame.

The Obama Administration held up the ARB report as the product of a full and complete investigation.

Since the ARB Report's release, the Administration has roundly praised it. President Obama said that the ARB "investigated every element" of the Benghazi attack.[30] In an appearance before the House Committee on Foreign Affairs, Secretary Clinton testified that had "great confidence that the Accountability Review Board did the job they were asked to do, made the recommendations that they thought were based on evidence, not on emotion."[31] Similarly, appearing before the Senate Committee on Foreign Relations, Deputy Secretary of State William Burns testified that the ARB report "takes a clear-eyed look at serious, systemic problems."[32]

Upon release of the unclassified ARB report, White House Press Secretary Jay Carney also praised the ARB for being "sophisticated in its analysis, blunt in its criticism, effective in its prescriptions."[33] Referring to the four Department officials relieved of their duties based on the ARB's findings, Carney stated, "there has already been, in this very short period of time, actions that demonstrate accountability as being upheld. . . . Immediately, accountability has been brought to bear with regard to four individuals who are very senior."[34]

In May 2013, Carney reiterated that the ARB conducted "a very rigorous investigation that reached a number of conclusions, including the fact that action was taken immediately and appropriately and that that action saved American lives."[35] State Department spokesman Patrick Ventrell was equally fulsome in his praise, citing "the ARB's credible, comprehensive process," which was "exhaustive and looked at these things in great detail. . . . The bottom line is the ARB looked at this in great depth."[36]

---

[30] The White House, Office of the Press Sec'y, Remarks by President Obama and Prime Minister Cameron of the United Kingdom in Joint Press Conference (May 13, 2013), http://www.whitehouse.gov/the-press-office/2013/05/13/remarks-president-obama-and-prime-minister-cameron-united-kingdom-joint-.

[31] *Terrorist Attack in Benghazi: The Secretary of State's View: Hearing Before the H. Comm. on Foreign Affairs*, 113th Cong., at 45 (Jan. 23, 2013) (testimony of Hon. Hillary Rodham Clinton, Sec'y, U.S. Dep't of State), http://docs.house.gov/meetings/FA/FA00/20130123/100170/HHRG-113-FA00-20130123-SD003.pdf.

[32] *Benghazi: The Attack and the Lessons Learned: Hearing Before the Senate Comm. on Foreign Relations*, 113th Cong. (Dec. 20, 2012) (Statement of Hon. William Burns, Deputy Sec'y, U.S. Dep't of State), http://www.foreign.senate.gov/imo/media/doc/William%20Burns%20Testimony.pdf._

[33] The White House, Office of the Press Sec'y, Press Briefing by Press Secretary Jay Carney (Dec. 20, 2012), http://www.whitehouse.gov/the-press-office/2012/12/20/press-briefing-press-secretary-jay-carney-12202012._

[34] *Id.*

[35] The White House, Office of the Press Sec'y, Press Briefing by Press Secretary Jay Carney (May 1, 2013), http://www.whitehouse.gov/the-press-office/2013/05/01/press-briefing-press-secretary-jay-carney-512013.

[36] U.S. Dep't of State, Daily Press Briefing, Patrick Ventrell, Acting Deputy Spokesperson (May 6, 2013), http://www.state.gov/r/pa/prs/dpb/2013/05/208988 htm#LIBYA.

Witnesses at the Committee's May 8, 2013 hearing raised questions about the ARB.

Despite the Administration's praise for the ARB Report, others have raised questions since its release. For example, the then-incoming Chairman of the House Committee on Foreign Affairs (HFAC), Ed Royce, stated, "The degree that others bear responsibility warrants congressional review, given the report's rather sweeping indictment."[37]

After appearances before the Senate Foreign Relations Committee and HFAC on December 19, 2012, Ambassador Pickering and Admiral Mullen declined invitations to appear before Congress to address concerns about the report. For example, on February 22, 2013, the Chairman of this Committee's Subcommittee on National Security, Jason Chaffetz, invited Ambassador Pickering and other members of the ARB to testify at a hearing on March 14, 2013. On March 1, 2013, an assistant for Admiral Michael Mullen, the Vice Chairman of the ARB, informed Committee staff that Admiral Mullen had declined to appear for any Benghazi-related hearing, and that Ambassador Pickering was coordinating a response with other members of the ARB. The same afternoon, Ambassador Pickering informed Committee staff that he had a previously scheduled conflict the day of the hearing. When asked if he would be available on another date, he conveyed that he was "deeply disinclined" to testify at any time because Congress had turned the issue into a "political circus."[38]

At the Committee's May 8, 2013 hearing on the Benghazi attacks, two witnesses raised questions as to whether the ARB was as effective in its work as some in the Administration apparently believed. Eric Nordstrom, the former Regional Security Officer at the U.S. Embassy in Tripoli, testified:

> Well, I guess the question that I have about the ARB -- and again, it's not what the ARB has. It's what it doesn't have and that it stops short of the very people that need to be asked those questions. And that's the Under Secretary of Management [Patrick F. Kennedy] and above. Those are perfect questions that he needs to answer.[39]

Nordstrom also testified:

> I go back to who authorized embassy employees, U.S. Government employees to go into facilities that did not meet legal requirements. I don't know who made that decision. And the reason why is because, as Ambassador Pickering said, he has decided to fix responsibility on the Assistant Secretary level and below. How I see that is, that's fine. It's an accountability of mid-level officer review board and the message to my colleagues is that **if you are above a certain level, no matter what your**

---

[37] Gordon & Schmitt, *supra* note 28.

[38] Teleconference between Ambassador Thomas Pickering and Committee Staff (Mar. 1, 2013).

[39] *Benghazi: Exposing Failure and Recognizing Courage: Hearing Before the H. Comm. on Oversight & Gov't Reform*, 113th Cong. (May 8, 2013), at 47 (testimony of Eric Nordstrom) [hereinafter "Exposing Failure"].

decision is, no one is going to question it. And that is my concern with the ARB.[40]

In an exchange with Congressman Tim Walberg, former Deputy Chief of Mission and Charge d'Affaires in Libya Gregory Hicks also expressed his view that the ARB may not have examined the upper echelons of the State Department's chain of command in assigning accountability for the management failures which contributed to the outcome of the Benghazi attack. Hicks testified:

> Q.   Do you think the ARB report lets any individual or bureaucracy off the hook?
>
> A. Again, as I mentioned earlier, given the decision-making that Under Secretary Pat Kennedy was making with respect to Embassy Tripoli and Consulate Benghazi operations, he has to bear some responsibility.[41]

Shortly before the Committee's May 8, 2013 hearing, and in the ensuing weeks, Ambassador Pickering and Admiral Mullen reversed course, announcing their desire to testify publicly before the Committee – despite their previous declinations.

The Committee welcomed their participation in a public hearing and began working with them to facilitate their testimony. To ensure that the hearing was fulsome and informed, the Committee requested the opportunity to conduct transcribed interviews with Ambassador Pickering and Admiral Mullen in advance of the hearing. The Committee conducted a deposition of Ambassador Pickering on June 4, 2013 and conducted a transcribed interview of Admiral Mullen on June 19, 2013. The Committee scheduled a hearing, entitled *Reviews of the Benghazi Attacks and Unanswered Questions*, on September 19, 2013, in order to give Members an opportunity to have an informed and constructive discussion with Ambassador Pickering and Admiral Mullen about concerns that have been raised about the ARB processes and conclusions. The hearing will also provide an opportunity to hear the views of members of the Independent Panel on Best Practices, which the State Department convened based on one of the ARB's 29 recommendations. Mark Sullivan, the Panel's chairman, as well as Todd Keil, a Panel member, will provide valuable insights about the review they conducted with the State Department's full support and cooperation.

---

[40] "Exposing Failure," at 56.
[41] "Exposing Failure," at 63 (testimony of Gregory Hicks).

The Committee's Investigation of the ARB

In light of questions raised prior to and during the May 8, 2013 hearing, the Committee expanded its investigation to include an evaluation of the ARB's processes, conclusions, and recommendations. Understanding the strengths and weaknesses of the ARB will help Congress ensure future ARBs are efficient and effective. The Committee's investigation seeks to assist the State Department in identifying areas in need of reform which the ARB may have overlooked.

Since the May 8, 2013 hearing, the Committee has interviewed more than a dozen current and former State Department employees. The majority of these witnesses serve in the two bureaus at the center of the ARB report – the Bureau of Near Eastern Affairs (NEA) and the Bureau of Diplomatic Security (DS). All officials the Committee has interviewed, including individuals placed on administrative leave as a result of the ARB's findings, complimented the ARB's professionalism. They described the ARB as "thorough,"[42] "professional"[43] and "well-prepared"[44] in their interviews. In addition, witnesses thought the report was "very tough,"[45] "factual,"[46] and would lead to "lasting improvement."[47] All of these witnesses, however, also provided testimony that raises questions about the process, procedures, and conclusions of the ARB.

There are weaknesses in the ARB's investigative process.

Shortly after the Secretary convened the ARB, the Board began the process of collecting documents and testimony to support its review. Admiral Mullen explained that the ARB cast a wide net and was willing to interview any and all witnesses relevant to its review. He stated:

> I had a discussion, private discussion with Ambassador Pickering about at least my expectation, and I would say this was in the first couple weeks, that this certainly could present the requirement that we would have to interview everybody up the chain of command, including the Secretary, and he agreed with that. So the two of us had sort of set that premise in terms of obviously depending on what we learned over time, and our requirement to both affix both responsibility and accountability per se were, again, based on the facts as we understood them. So there was a consensus, and it was a universal consensus over time that we did the interviews we needed to do and that we didn't do the interviews we didn't do, which would have included the ones obviously that we didn't do, which were Nides and Burns and Secretary Clinton.[48]

---

[42] Transcribed Interview of Eric Boswell, Transcript at 79 (July 9, 2013) [hereinafter Boswell Tr.]; Transcribed Inteview of Beth Jones, Transcript at 95 (July 11, 2013) [hereinafter Jones Tr.].
[43] Boswell Tr. at 81.
[44] *Id.* at 79.
[45] Jones Tr. at 95.
[46] Transcribed Interview of Elizabeth Dibble, Transcript at 72 (July 10, 2013) [hereinafter Dibble Tr.].
[47] Jones Tr. at 106.
[48] Mullen Tr. at 26-27.

The Board had the authority both to conduct depositions and require interrogatories.[49] The ARB also had the authority to issue subpoenas for testimony and documents.[50] The Board never exercised these authorities.[51] It conducted both group and individual interviews. The ARB also recalled some of the officials who participated in group interviews for individual interviews. For example, Scott Bultrowicz appeared before the Board on three separate occasions. He stated:

> I had three appearances with the ARB. The first one was shortly after it convened. Myself, Assistant Secretary Boswell, and Deputy Assistant Secretary Lamb, provided an overview brief of what we knew at the time, facts surrounding the attack itself. And I can't recall the date that we did that. My second appearance was my one-on-one with the ARB, and that was, I believe in late November that I received notification, time, date, place, and time to arrive. And then the third appearance was actually with only two of the panel members and it was myself, and the acting Chief Information Officer from State. They had some follow-up questions on a classified issue that they needed answers to. So that sort of, in general, was my interaction with the ARB.[52]

Other witnesses only appeared once before the Board. For example, Elizabeth Dibble, the second-most senior official in NEA—one of the two bureaus the ARB criticized—only appeared once before the ARB as part of a group interview that lasted about an hour and a half. When asked specifically about Dibble, Admiral Mullen stated, "[she] never really got up on the scope, per se, in terms of visibility, in terms of responsibility, what she did or did not do, from my perspective."[53] The fact that the second most senior person in NEA—a bureau the ARB ultimately cited for "systemic leadership and management deficiencies,"[54]—appeared once, as part of a group and for less than two hours, raises a number of questions about the thoroughness of the ARB's review. For example, aside from her participation in the short group interview, it is still unclear what information the ARB reviewed that led to the conclusion that her role or awareness of issues related to Benghazi did not warrant further inquiry.

In fact, the Committee has reviewed numerous documents that suggest that Dibble was involved in discussions about the U.S. presence in Benghazi and security resources deployed in Libya. In addition, individuals and offices under her direct supervision were involved in the coordination of security resources with DS and the U.S. mission in Benghazi. Regardless of her role or responsibility for decisions related to the security posture in Benghazi, both her involvement in e-mail traffic and references to her made by others in e-mail exchanges raise questions about which, if any, of these documents the ARB reviewed or discussed with Dibble.

---

[49] 22 U.S.C. § 4833(a)(1).

[50] Id. § 4833(a)(3).

[51] Pickering Tr. at 17.

[52] Transcribed Interview of Scott Bultrowicz, Transcript at 72-73 (July 8, 2013) [hereinafter Bultrowicz Tr.].

[53] Mullen Tr. at 38.

[54] ARB Report at 4.

The State Department's refusal to turn over documents and materials reviewed by the ARB has limited the Committee's ability to evaluate the thoroughness and accuracy of the ARB process. Without access to this information, the Committee is forced to rely on the recollections of ARB members and State Department employees the ARB interviewed. Witnesses' recollections of events that occurred many months ago are understandably limited. For example, Admiral Mullen could not recall any specific documentation that supported the ARB's finding regarding Ray Maxwell. He testified:

> Q. [D]id the board members look at the documentary evidence about Maxwell's role in working with the people in Libya, communicating their concerns about security and working with DS in Washington about bridging that gap?
>
> A. I'm not sure. I mean -- I don't recall one way or the other.
>
> Q. Whether the paper trail supports his role in that?
>
> A. I just don't recall.[55]

Admiral Mullen also could not recall reviewing any documents relevant to other senior employees within NEA. He stated:

> Q. And do you know if Dibble or Jones were showing up in the documents as participants in the documentary traffic on what was happening in Libya?
>
> A. I don't. I don't.[56]

In addition, the Committee has been unable to assess with any specificity what information witnesses conveyed to the ARB during interviews. The ARB did not maintain official transcripts of the testimony provided to the Board. Instead, it developed reports of each interview based on the notes of staff and Board members. Mullen testified:

> Q. How were the interviews recorded? Was there a court reporter? Was there video? Was there audio recording? Note taking?
>
> A. Note taking.
>
> Q. And none of the other options?
>
> A. No.
>
> Q. And how did it get put together?

---

[55] Mullen Tr. at 110-11.
[56] *Id.* at 47.

A. The staff would put a summary of the interview together. We would -- the members would be able to review that summary shortly after the interview.

Q.   Any concerns with that?

A.   No.

Q.   That it wasn't transcribed or recorded?

A. No. From the standpoint of content, substance and content, I found them to be very accurate.[57]

The State Department has steadfastly refused to turn over these records to the Committee. Without access to the notes Admiral Mullen described, the Committee cannot verify claims that these interviews were, in fact, thorough. Witnesses' recollections of their discussions with the ARB have been spotty and, at times, extremely limited. For example, when asked whether she recalled the content of her individual interview with the ARB, Ambassador Jones stated, "Not really. It was more detail on the same kinds of things. I don't remember the detail at all."[58]

Testimony the Committee has obtained through its own interviews raises questions about the substance of individual ARB interviews. Scott Bultrowicz, one of the individuals the ARB cited for accountability, told the Committee that the ARB never questioned him about issues for which it later criticized him. He testified:

A. I mean, what I sort of found odd is I thought maybe there would be more, you know, direct questions about Benghazi itself.

Q. It struck you as odd that that was such a small portion of the questioning?

A. Well, in hindsight, you know, after the ARB's release and me being relieved of my duties, I myself would think, okay, if I'm being relieved, I would have appreciated maybe a little bit more direct questioning as to my role in supervising a subordinate or proactive steps that I took in regards to Benghazi, which I understand were sort of the two main issues for me.[59]

Ambassador Boswell also told the Committee that the ARB did not ask him any questions about the actions of his subordinates or his supervision of them. He stated:

A. I do remember that there was no questioning about my role as a supervisor, none at all. There was no indication of what

_____

[57] *Id.* at 29-30.
[58] Jones Tr. at 94.
[59] Bultrowicz Tr. at 76.

conclusions the ARB was coming to, not a clue of any of these, any conclusions. And there was -- as I say, I was talking about what was not asked -- there was no conversation about my supervision. I don't remember any -- as I mentioned before, any conversation about confusion as to who was in charge of what, stovepiping, lack of transparency. And at the end of the meeting, we shook hands warmly, and Tom Pickering gave me a big hug because I've known him for a long time, and I left. **And I was absolutely stunned when I saw the report.**

Q.   So no questions about the actions of your subordinates, or your role in supervising them, or anything --

A.   Not that I recall, no.[60]

If the ARB did not question supervisors about the actions of their subordinates, or even discuss their awareness or supervision of those actions, it is unclear how the Board reached its conclusions regarding accountability for these individuals. The Committee's investigation seeks answers to these questions to ensure that the ARB process envisioned by the statute is truly efficient and effective. Otherwise, convening an ARB is a pointless exercise.

There are weaknesses in the ARB's independence.

The Committee has reviewed documents and obtained witness testimony that calls into question whether the ARB process and structure give the Board the independence necessary to conduct an objective and fair evaluation. As currently structured, the ARB is heavily reliant on the State Department for personnel and resources. The Secretary convenes the ARB and nominates four of five members, and the Department provides the necessary staff and resources. Such heavy reliance on State Department employees and resources has the potential to create not only the appearance of a conflict of interest, but also actual conflicts. For example, Under Secretary for Management Patrick Kennedy supervised the selection of the Benghazi ARB staff. This placed the staff in a position in which their duties required them to evaluate the performance of supervisors, colleagues, and friends. Additionally, two ARB members selected by Secretary Clinton–Ambassador Pickering and Richard Shinnick–had extensive experience with the State Department. Although a third member of the ARB, Catherine Bertini, did not come from the State Department, Pickering recommended her for the Board. He stated:

Q.   And did you have any role in the selection of the other members?

A.   I was asked for my ideas, and I provided my ideas, yes.

Q.   And were any of the individuals that you -- did you recommend any specific individuals?

_____

[60] Boswell at 32-33 (emphasis added).

A.   I did, yes.

Q.   And who did you recommend?

A.   The one that I recall who has served, did serve on the board was Catherine Bertini.

Q.   Any of the other?

A.   I made other recommended names. None of them appeared on the board. I was asked by Mr. Kennedy for those thoughts.[61]

Witnesses rejected the notion that the current structure—heavily dictated by the Department—compromised the independence of the Benghazi review. In fact, ARB Vice-Chair Admiral Michael Mullen considered the Board's familiarity with State Department protocol and personnel to be helpful. Admiral Mullen testified:

Q.   The ARB is supposed to be set up as an independent review board. Did you have any questions about the independence of the board?

A.   In fact, in the original conversation I had with Ms. Mills about this, from my perspective, the most important descriptive characteristic of it is that it would be independent, and Ms. Mills assured me that was the Secretary's intent upfront, and had that not been the case, I certainly wouldn't have agreed to it. Secondly, I saw in execution that independence throughout, from beginning to end, that it was supported. We had the authority to, within the scope of the tasking, to do just about anything that we thought was important with respect to that tasking.[62]

* * *

Q.   Did you ever see any question as to whether that State Department heavy component played into any of the board's work?

A.   It played into, from my perspective, a depth and a breadth of knowledge in terms of how the State Department functions, what the culture is, what was reasonable in terms of expectations in certain situations that we would examine, and I found it to be -- as much as I had worked with the State Department, particularly as Chairman, it's one thing to be outside an organization and work with, it's quite different to be inside to try to understand the inner

---

[61] Pickering Tr. at 12.
[62] Mullen Tr. at 19.

24

workings and hidden mechanisms of a massive organization like that. So in that regard they were incredibly helpful.[63]

Mullen subsequently described, however, an example of how a culture of collegiality could undermine the ARB's independence. Mullen put Cheryl Mills on notice in advance of her interview that the Board's questions could be "difficult" for the State Department. He stated:

Q. During the life of the board, did you or any of the board members update State Department officials or DOD officials about the work of the board that you know of?

A.   With respect to DOD, no. Shortly after we interviewed Ms. Lamb, I initiated a call to Ms. Mills to give her -- what I wanted to give her was a head's up because at this point she was on the list to come over here to testify, and I was -- so from a department representation standpoint and as someone that led a department, I always focused on certainly trying to make sure the best witnesses were going to appear before the department, and my reaction at that point in time with Ms. Lamb at the interview was -- and it was a pretty unstable time. It was the beginning, there was a lot of unknowns. To the best of my knowledge, she hadn't appeared either ever or many times certainly. So essentially I gave Ms. Mills a head's up that **I thought that her appearance could be a very difficult appearance for the State Department, and that was about** -- that was the extent of the conversation.[64]

Admiral Mullen's testimony calls the ARB's independence into question, as it creates the appearance that a member of an independent body is placing the interests or reputation of the entity under investigation above the body's investigative mandate.

Furthermore, the State Department's attempts to characterize the ARB as independent have proven to be inconsistent with the Department's action in response to the congressional investigation of the Benghazi attacks. In refusing to produce ARB materials subpoenaed by the Committee, the State Department has sought to compare the ARB to "analogous investigative bodies such as Offices of Inspectors General."[65] If an Inspector General, however, encouraged agency leaders to prevent a witness from testifying before Congress because that witness's testimony could reflect poorly on the Department, the Inspector General's credibility would be greatly diminished. An ARB should be held to the same standard, if the State Department is to use the community of Inspectors General as a point of reference.

Testimony provided by other witnesses suggests that the State Department's culture complicates the perception of the ARB's independence. Senior State Department officials often

---

[63] *Id.* at 19-20.
[64] *Id.* at 23-24.
[65] Letter from Thomas B. Gibbons, Acting Ass't Sec., Leg. Affairs, U.S. Dep't of State, to Hon. Darrell E. Issa, Chairman, H. Comm. on Oversight & Gov't Reform (Aug. 23, 2013).

work together and develop close connections throughout their careers in the Foreign Service. For example, Ambassador Jones expressed no concerns about the independence of the Board while also describing her previous interactions with current and former State Department employees working on the ARB. She stated:

> Q. Had you had any professional interaction or relationships with the members or the staff of the ARB? I know a lot of them came from State.
>
> A. Yes. The person who was appointed as executive director, I guess she was called, of the ARB, Uzra Zeya, was someone I knew quite well having been the chief of staff to the deputy secretary until fairly recently, so I had had daily interactions with her, and I've known her through the years because she came out of NEA. Dick Shinnick, who was on the ARB, is someone I had known for many years. I never worked directly with him, we never served at a post together, but he was the kind of person one just knew because he was in jobs that we all had interactions with at various times. Ambassador Pickering was my ambassador in Jordan when I was the junior political officer in Amman in the 1970s, and I worked for him then for a year before the new ambassador came in. And then, when he was under secretary for political affairs and I was the principal deputy assistant secretary for NEA, I had interactions with him then. I didn't report directly to him either time but we had reason to be in meetings together and that kind of thing.[66]

* * *

> A. On Ambassador Pickering, when I was in the private sector I served on two boards, two nonprofit boards with Ambassador Pickering.
>
> Q. And that was the period immediately before coming back to the State Department?
>
> A. Correct.[67]

Numerous witnesses described similar professional connections to ARB members, staff or colleagues within the State Department. For example, Maxwell testified that Shinnick had a number of connections with senior State Department officials, including with Maxwell himself. Maxwell stated:

> Dick Shinnick was connected to Lee Loman. Dick Shinnick was connected to Pat Kennedy, a long-term series of overlapping assignments

---

[66] Jones Tr. at 162-163.
[67] *Id.* at 163-164.

and connections. For that matter, I was connected to them all as well. We were all management officers, and--management officers back home by trade.[68]

Some of these connections were well known to State Department employees. Lee Lohman told the Committee that he was aware of the extensive connections between Ambassador Pickering, Richard Shinnick and current State Department employees. He stated:

> Thomas Pickering spent his entire career at the State Department and Richard Shinnick as well, so they knew all of the players, or many of the players anyway. And Thomas Pickering, obviously, knew -- well, I shouldn't say obviously, but he knew Beth Jones, and I think he knew Ms. Dibble.[69]

While a culture of mentoring and collegiality within the State Department has obvious benefits, such an environment also fortifies institutional priorities and organizational structures that are resistant to change. For example, in the wake of the 1998 attacks on the U.S. embassies in Kenya and Tanzania, the State Department implemented a number of changes recommended by the ARB chaired by Admiral William Crowe. The Department did not, however, adopt any significant changes that altered existing reporting lines or organizational structures. Most notably, an external review conducted by Booz Allen Hamilton recommended systemic changes at the State Department – specifically, the elevation of the Diplomatic Security function to the level of Under Secretary.[70] Despite initial support for this recommendation and the approval of then-Secretary of State Madeleine Albright, it was never realized.

Similarly, following the Benghazi attacks, the State Department readily accepted the recommendations of the State Department-commissioned ARB. Ambassador Pickering told the Committee that he was "deeply concerned, as others were, that previous ARBs, previous Accountability Review Boards, had been excellent in their recommendations, but the follow-through had dwindled away."[71] Despite his stated concern –and the parallels between the institutional failures identified with the 1998 attacks and what transpired leading up to the attacks in Benghazi – the Benghazi ARB downplayed the significance of decisions above the bureau level. As such, the ARB's recommendations focused on improving processes and coordination within the existing organization, as opposed to recommending significant structural and organizational changes.

While the Benghazi ARB did not recommend the type of significant change Booz Allen had recommended in 1999, it did recommend an evaluation by external security experts—the Best Practices Panel. This Panel proposed similar, if not identical, changes as Booz Allen had over a decade earlier. For example, both panels proposed elevating the security function within

---

[68] Transcribed Interview of Ray Maxwell, Transcript at 36 (May 30, 2013) [hereinafter Maxwell Tr.].
[69] Transcribed Interview of Lee Lohman, Transcript at 110 (July 30, 2013) [hereinafter Lohman Tr.].
[70] *See* Trevor Aaronson, *Exclusive: Benghazi report details security flaws at US diplomatic posts*, AL JAZEERA AMERICA, Sept. 3, 2013, http://america.aljazeera.com/articles/2013/9/3/exclusive-benghazireportdetailssecurityflawsatusdiplomaticposts.html.
[71] Pickering Tr. at 56-57.

the Department through the creation of an Under Secretary for Diplomatic Security.[72] In addition, the Best Practices report made clear that the creation of this position was "crucial to the successful and sustainable implantation" of all of its recommendations.[73] However, the Panel worried that the State Department—under the leadership of many of the same employees who failed to implement Booz Allen's recommendations over a decade earlier[74]—would once again fail to actually implement the proposed changes. The Panel explained that although the Department had received a "significant amount" of best practices input since the creation of DS, it routinely failed to adapt and implement recommendations as to best practices.[75]

The Best Practices Panel, which made forty security-related recommendations to the Department, found a complete lack of accountability and management at the Department level. The Panel found that Department employees did not understand the security-related responsibilities of their colleagues.[76] Further, the Department had no formal risk management system in place to balance program criticality and acceptable risk. As a result, there was no clear way for Department officials to determine if the level of risk at the Benghazi mission was acceptable.[77] The Panel found that the Department did not even have a formalized "hot wash," or after-action debriefing process of key participants following major events.[78] In fact, as of the date of the Best Practices Report, apart from the ARB and Best Practice Panel interviews, no Department bureau or office — not even DS itself — had debriefed DS Agents who survived the attack in Benghazi for lessons learned.[79] The Panel also observed that the State Department created policies and procedures, only to issue waivers when its "expeditionary diplomacy" demanded facilities and missions that did not meet those standards.[80]

The Committee recognizes the likelihood that the Department will once again pay lip-service to the recommendations of the Best Practices Panel, as it has done to similar independent panels in the past, but not take the concrete steps necessary to bring about badly-needed change. Many of the same people in positions of authority and responsibility following the Booz Allen

---

[72] Report of the Independent Panel on Best Practices, U.S. Dep't of State, at 5 [hereinafter Best Practices Report].

[73] Best Practices Report at i.

[74] *See supra* note 70.

[75] *Id.* at 26. The report states:

> In the 27 years since DS' creation, the Department has received a significant amount of best practice input from 18 ARBs and a number of independent panels, such as the current one. . . .The panel observes that the challenge for the Department and DS has not been in obtaining regular best practice and SME input, but in incorporating that knowledge into operations and management capabilities.

[76] The Best Practices Panel Report contrasts the complete lack of understanding of lines of authority and security responsibilities of Department employees with the clear understanding of lines of authority and security responsibilities by those serving outside of the Department under the authority of Chiefs of Mission. Further, Department employees could not identify the senior security executive ultimately responsible for safety and security, the Assistant Secretary for Diplomatic Security, instead often naming the Under Secretary for Management as the senior security official. *Id.* at 3.

[77] *Id.* at 8-10.

[78] *Id.* at 13.

[79] *Id.* at 14.

[80] *See, e.g.*, Best Practices Report at 12 ("The Panel is therefore concerned that minimum operating security standards would also be established and then waived.").

report remain influential in the Department today.[81] The Department's failure to implement the recommendations of several independent panels over the years is consistent with the Department's current failure to recognize the shortcomings of the ARB process that it has implemented and controlled.

The ARB's findings and recommendations had weaknesses.

Many witnesses the Committee interviewed praised the ARB's recommendations, as well as the Department's implementation of them. Ambassador Elizabeth Jones, the Acting Assistant Secretary for NEA, told the Committee:

Q.   [...] Do you feel that this ARB does enough to help ensure these are lasting improvements?

A. I think it does, not least because -- well, both because the recommendations are detailed and easy to understand. They're well documented. They're well explained, and because of the system that was implemented immediately to understand each of the recommendations, to break them down into the 65 from the 29, and assign responsibility for completing each of the recommendations, and meeting on a very regular basis with everybody who was involved with any part of it so we all knew what everybody else was doing and knew how everything we were trying to do fit in, and so we could have discussions about, okay, if the goal is to break down the impression, or the fact that DS is hard to engage with, what kinds of things do we all think would work and be appropriate to make fulfilling that recommendation a lasting improvement.

Q. So you think it goes beyond just providing, say, brick and mortar solutions to security?

A.   Yes.[82]

Jones' former counterpart at Diplomatic Security, Eric Boswell – whom the ARB singled out for criticism – nonetheless found value in the ARB's contribution to understanding the environment in which his bureau had been operating. He stated:

---

[81] Not surprisingly, a number of senior officials involved in events before, during and after the attacks on Benghazi – including the ARB – held senior positions within the Department prior to, and after, the 1998 attacks. At the time, Thomas Pickering was the Under Secretary for Political Affairs. Patrick Kennedy was the Assistant Secretary for the Bureau of Administration. He also served in concurrent positions in the years leading up to the 1998 attacks. From 1996-1997 he was the Acting Under Secretary for Management – the position he currently holds – and in 1998 he was the Acting Assistant Secretary for Diplomatic Security. Eric Boswell, who served in the latter position from 1996 until January 1998, served in that same role at the time of the attacks in Benghazi. In addition, Susan Rice was Assistant Secretary for the Bureau of African Affairs.
[82] Jones Tr. at 105-106.

I think the ARB got many things right, starting with the accountability for what happened in Benghazi lies with the terrorists; they are the people that are responsible. That's finding number 1. I think the ARB accurately portrayed the environment that DS was operating in not just in Benghazi, but worldwide, and the shift of the environment in which DS and the State Department was operating from historic times, the fact that we are practicing expeditionary diplomacy and the increasing demands on DS.[83]

Along with this praise, though, these individuals and others questioned a number of the ARB's findings and recommendations.

The ARB found "systemic failures and leadership and management deficiencies" in two bureaus but downplayed the decisions by senior State Department officials to run the Benghazi mission on an *ad hoc* basis.

The ARB's central finding with respect to the failures that led to the tragedy in Benghazi focused on two bureaus within the State Department: the Bureau of Diplomatic Security within the Under Secretariat for Management and the Bureau of Near Eastern Affairs within the Under Secretariat for Political Affairs.[84] The ARB found that:

> Systemic failures and leadership and management deficiencies at senior levels within two bureaus of the State Department . . . resulted in a Special Mission security posture that was inadequate for Benghazi and grossly inadequate to deal with the attack that took place.[85]

The ARB Report accurately identified a number of failures which contributed to an insufficient security posture at the Benghazi special mission compound. These failures included a temporary staffing model using an inadequate number of security personnel and the failure of the Department's Washington headquarters to provide the requested level of security personnel. The Report stated:

> Overall, the number of Bureau of Diplomatic Security (DS) security staff in Benghazi on the day of the attack and in the months and weeks leading up to it was inadequate, despite repeated requests from Special Mission Benghazi and Embassy Tripoli for additional staffing.[86]

The Committee's investigation corroborates these ARB findings. Like the Committee, the ARB determined that a major contributing factor to these failures was the temporary and *ad hoc* nature of the U.S. diplomatic mission in Benghazi. According to the ARB:

---

[83] Boswell Tr. at 81.
[84] Mullen Tr. at 107.
[85] ARB Report at 4.
[86] ARB Report at 5.

Special Mission Benghazi's uncertain future after 2012 and its 'non-status' as a temporary, residential facility made allocation of resources for security and personnel more difficult, and left responsibility to meet security standards to the working-level in the field, with very limited resources;[87]

* * *

The short-term, transitory nature of Special Mission Benghazi's staffing, with talented and committed, but relatively inexperienced, American personnel often on temporary assignments of 40 days or less, resulted in diminished institutional knowledge, continuity, and mission capacity.[88]

The ARB, however, downplayed the importance of the Department's leadership and organizational structure as the source of the decision to run the Benghazi mission on an *ad hoc* basis. Indeed, it was a particularly ill-defended outpost of what the Department has labeled "expeditionary diplomacy." None of the four individuals the ARB singled out for "accountability" made this decision. Rather, it could accurately be described as "above their pay grade." Therefore, while the ARB correctly identified the symptoms of the Benghazi failure, it failed to identify accurately the individuals, organizations, and policies that led to these symptoms.

The Diplomatic Security Bureau

The Committee's investigation shows that the ARB's focus on DS was understandable. The Committee obtained witness testimony confirming that DS was the bureau most immediately responsible for security-related planning and resource allocation for the two U.S. diplomatic posts in Libya—the Embassy in Tripoli and the Special Mission Compound in Benghazi. While many of the ARB's findings rightly point to shortcomings that manifested themselves in areas within the DS Bureau's area of responsibility, the Committee's investigation raises questions about whether the ARB looked high enough within the State Department organizational chart when assigning accountability for the failures it identified. In fact, the Committee's investigation suggests that with respect to several important failures, DS was constrained by decisions made by the Department's senior leadership, particularly within the Under Secretariat for Management.

Special Mission Benghazi: An Unfunded Mandate

Documents and testimony obtained by the Committee show that DS struggled to provide adequate resources both to protect the Benghazi compound and allow the diplomats stationed there to move outside the walls and perform their intended mission. The ARB made a similar

---

[87] ARB Report at 5.
[88] ARB Report at 4.

finding. The documents and testimony show that one of the major contributing factors to this deficiency was the temporary nature of the Benghazi compound authorized by Under Secretary Patrick Kennedy. The ARB downplayed Kennedy's role in the decision-making that led to the inadequate security posture in Benghazi.

Once the U.S. reopened its embassy in Tripoli in September 2011, the center of gravity of U.S. diplomatic activity shifted away from Benghazi to Tripoli. As a result, the future of the Benghazi special mission compound, which had never been an official U.S. diplomatic facility, was uncertain. The property lease for the Benghazi mission was due to expire in early February 2012. And, according to e-mails reviewed by the Committee, as late as December 2011 many State Department employees both in Washington and in Benghazi remained uncertain as to whether the mission would close when the lease expired.

Finally, in December 2011, then-Assistant Secretary for Near Eastern Affairs Jeffrey Feltman sent an Action Memorandum to Under Secretary for Management Patrick Kennedy, requesting that Kennedy "approve a continued U.S. presence in Benghazi through the end of calendar year 2012."[89] The memo cited ongoing U.S. policy interests in maintaining a State Department footprint in Benghazi, including the need to maintain political, economic, public diplomacy, and commercial reporting in eastern Libya, a historically marginalized but politically and economically important part of Libya. According to the memo, "Many Libyans have said the U.S. presence in Benghazi has a salutary, calming effect on easterners who are fearful that the new focus on Tripoli could once again lead to their neglect and exclusion from reconstruction and wealth distribution and strongly favor a permanent U.S. presence in the form of a full consulate."[90]

Kennedy approved the memo, extending the Benghazi special mission compound's life for one year, through the end of December 2012. Rather than the "full consulate" envisioned by the Libyans, however, the Benghazi compound was a "temporary, residential facility, not officially notified to the host government, even though it was also a full time office facility."[91] This ad hoc status created challenges for DS, which struggled to provide the necessary security resources to operate the facility safely. In fact, the senior official who provided DS clearance on the memo prior to its transmittal to Under Secretary Kennedy anticipated this challenge. According to an e-mail dated December 23, 2011, the acting Principal Deputy Assistant Secretary cleared the memo "with the comment that this operation continues to be an unfunded mandate and a drain on personnel resources."[92]

The DS desk officer for Libya explained:

[A]s a temporary facility, not a U.S. mission, [an] accredited . . . embassy or consulate . . . everything that was provided to it had to come from somewhere else, someplace that something was already allotted to essentially. So, for funding, at least in my experience, we would have to

---

[89] Jeffrey Feltman, "Action Memo for Under Secretary Kennedy – M" (Dec. 27, 2011) [hereinafter Feltman Memo].
[90] Feltman Memo.
[91] ARB Report at 30.
[92] State Department Production, Document No. C05427113 (Aug. 2013).

draw from other sources within DS/IP/NEA for other programs that we were supposed to be doing. And for personnel, in my experience, the agent pool that I pulled from mostly was from domestic operations. And they have a mission as well which they are supposed to be doing. So we had to pull them from that as well.[93]

It has been suggested by the State Department and some Members of Congress that budget cuts caused a shortfall in resources, which led to inadequate security at the Benghazi special mission compound. Documents and testimony show that the State Department budget did not affect the security posture in Benghazi. In fact, the "non-status" of the Benghazi compound appears to have been the most important factor. Charlene Lamb testified:

> Q. It has been suggested that budget cuts were responsible for a lack of security in Benghazi. I would like to ask, Ms. Lamb, you made this decision personally; was there any budget consideration and lack of budget which led you not to increase the number of people in the security force there?
>
> A. No, sir.[94]

The effect of the mission's temporary status manifested itself in a number of ways.

Personnel Security

According to the action memorandum signed by Kennedy, which extended the Benghazi mission, DS would provide a "full complement of five Special Agents" to protect two NEA diplomats and a communications officer.[95] Having an appropriate number of agents would allow for the protection of the compound and permit the necessary security support to allow diplomats stationed there to travel off-compound in order to fulfill the mission's diplomatic purpose. According to the ARB, however, the Benghazi special mission had its full complement of five DS agents for only 23 days between January 1 and September 9, 2013.[96]

With a permanent diplomatic post, the DS Bureau is able to engage in its normal long-term planning for budgets and personnel. These posts are staffed by full-time equivalent Regional Security Officers (RSO) from the regular pool of DS agents.[97] In contrast, temporary duty assignment (TDY) agents staffed temporary facilities such as Tripoli and Benghazi. Pulled from their existing assignments, these TDY agents and were thrust into an environment for which they often had not trained adequately. Charlene Lamb's Diplomatic Security/International Programs (DS/IP) office ran this TDY staffing system, rather than the normal pool of agents. It

---

[93] Transcribed Interview of Brian Papanu, Transcript at 94 (Aug. 8, 2013) [hereinafter Papanu Tr.].

[94] *The Security Failures of Benghazi, Hearing Before the H. Comm. on Oversight & Gov't Reform*, 113th Cong., at 149 (Oct. 10, 2012) (testimony of Charlene Lamb, U.S. Dep't of State).

[95] Feltman Memo.

[96] ARB Report at 31.

[97] Papanu Tr. at 18-19.

was never designed to provide the long-term staffing needed in Libya. Rather, the TDY system was designed as a stop-gap to fill short-term vacancies at post due to temporary absences of permanently-assigned personnel. Brian Papanu, the Libya desk officer in DS/IP/NEA explained the challenges in the year leading up to the Benghazi attack to the Committee. He stated:

Q. Do you know why there was difficulty getting to five or why there were so infrequently five agents [in Benghazi]?

A. Yes.

Q. Can you explain?

A. Certainly. In October of 2011, I assumed responsibilities for obtaining TDY staff for all of Libya. Prior to that, it was a desk officer colleague of mine. The mission in -- around the same time, September, October, the mission in Benghazi changed essentially from a protection mission, which was run by our dignitary protection unit here in Washington, to a more traditional RSO program management position, which pushed it back into DS/IP's, my office's realm. So at that time the mechanism to get agents changed, they have a task-oriented system, we have a -- it's hard to describe, but it's a system where basically we get volunteers to go. It's usually the high threat posts. And our system is, generally we cover -- traditionally we cover one RSO position like over a summer transition or during a break. It was very difficult for us to get the type of numbers on kind of a continuous basis through the volunteer system.

Q. [I]t sounds like you're alluding that the system was kind of designed to deal with one absence here or one absence there, but is that because typically with a traditional RSO model you've got a more regular staffing kind of already set up and you're just kind of staffing the gaps, like during vacations in August or something like that?

A. That's correct. Typically we just cover the gaps, but we did do -- occasionally we would do -- particularly in the beginning of Arab spring, it was very busy, and we had to find TDY support. But generally it wasn't near that number. It was never near that number. And it was for a much shorter timeframe, usually only one or two 60- to 30-day deployments for agents.

Q. So is it fair to say that Benghazi being a sort of a non-official post but still needed a significant number of TDY agents, that sort of created challenges for you guys in staffing that, given your model?

34

A.   **Definitely**.[98]

To provide sufficient DS staffing for Libya, the TDY staffing system was entirely dependent on volunteers both willing and able to take a leave of absence from their permanent assignments for TDY assignments in Libya. Papanu testified:

> A.   [A]s a high-threat post, in DS/IP, we would take only volunteers. And as a volunteer, the people that were interested in attending would not only have to volunteer themselves, they would also have to get their superiors and potentially their superior's superiors to sign off on the TDY, which could be a significant amount of time away from whatever their current duties were. So that was one of the other factors.[99]
>
> * * *
>
> There is no pool. There is not agents waiting to be grabbed to go that are standing by, at least agents that I was deploying, the TDY agents.[100]

In preparation for a July 2, 2012, meeting with Under Secretary Kennedy, Ambassador Eric Boswell, Assistant Secretary for Diplomatic Security, instructed Charlene Lamb to ensure that the DS representative reiterated the Bureau's concerns with the staffing challenges and security conditions in Benghazi:

> Re the Benghazi item, DS should express its concern over the resource drain that the endless TDYs in Benghazi in inflicting on us, and also concern that the overall security situation in Libya, Tripoli included, is deteriorating. We can't keep up these TDYs indefinitely. And having said that, if we are required to keep going in Benghazi we must salute and do it.[101]

Physical Security

Another area where the ARB correctly identified a security shortcoming of the Benghazi special mission compound, yet failed to assign appropriate accountability, was with respect to the post's failure to meet State Department physical security standards. The unclassified ARB Report found that:

---

[98] *Id.* at 18-19 (emphasis added).
[99] *Id.* at 50.
[100] *Id.* at 95.
[101] E-mail from Eric J. Boswell to Charlene R. Lamb, "FW: AGENDA for NEA-SCA EX Meeting with US Kennedy – 7/2/12" (June 29, 2012, 3:48 p m.).

The insufficient Special Mission security platform was at variance with the appropriate Overseas Security Policy Board (OSPB) standards with respect to perimeter and interior security. Benghazi was also severely under-resourced with regard to certain needed security equipment, although DS funded and installed in 2012 a number of physical security upgrades.[102]

The ARB Report further elaborates that, as with personnel shortfalls, the special mission compound's physical security was a direct casualty of the decision to operate it as a temporary facility:

> Another key driver behind the weak security platform in Benghazi was the decision to treat Benghazi as a temporary, residential facility, not officially notified to the host government, even though it was also a full time office facility. This resulted in the Special Mission compound being excepted from office facility standards and accountability under the Secure Embassy Construction and Counterterrorism Act of 1999 (SECCA) and the Overseas Security Policy Board (OSPB). Benghazi's initial platform in November 2011 was far short of OSPB standards and remained so even in September 2012, despite multiple field-expedient upgrades funded by DS. (As a temporary, residential facility, SMC was not eligible for OBO-funded security upgrades.) A comprehensive upgrade and risk-mitigation plan did not exist, nor was a comprehensive security review conducted by Washington for Benghazi in 2012. The unique circumstances surrounding the creation of the mission in Benghazi as a temporary mission outside the realm of permanent diplomatic posts resulted in significant disconnects and support gaps.[103]

Documents and testimony obtained by the Committee show that the exemption of the Benghazi special mission compound from Department physical security guidelines was not the result of a decision made by any of the four individuals singled out for "accountability" by the ARB. In fact, the Under Secretary for Management approved the decision to allow U.S. diplomats to move into an "as-is" facility.

Normally, an interim or permanent diplomatic post must request a waiver in order to operate under an exception to OSPB physical security standards. The Committee asked the former Principal Deputy Assistant Secretary and Director of the Diplomatic Security Service, Scott Bultrowicz, about the procedure for requesting waivers from OSPB standards. He testified:

> The OSPB standards, those could be signed off by the Assistant Secretary, the waiver of OSPB standards.
>
> But there's an important element into that, in that the waiver packet, that is

---

[102] ARB Report at 5.
[103] *Id.* at 30-31.

produced by post. So post has to go and they have to do a physical security survey, identify what standards are being met, which ones aren't being met, which ones can we meet with upgrades, and which ones we just won't be able to meet, and those would have to be the ones that would be waived.

In that packet, there would also be a statement from the Ambassador stating that he has reviewed the survey, he has reviewed what requires being waived, and he is in agreement with that based upon foreign policy priorities and objectives.

And that would also be accompanied by a statement from the RSO stating that he or she is cognizant of the facilities, the physical security footprint, what needs to be upgraded, what can't be upgraded, and that they're in support of these waivers.

That's brought back to Washington. It's reviewed. And where the upgrades could not be made, the waiver packet would go forward.[104]

According to Boswell, OSPB standards did not apply to Benghazi because of its status as a temporary facility:

[I]n my opinion, the standards apply to permanent facilities, not temporary ones. Having said that, as I mentioned previously, in any place we have people we do our best to get as close, because OSPB standard is the standard for us, it's the gold standard, and we try to get as close as we can to it.[105]

In Ambassador Boswell's view, the entire Department was aware that Benghazi did not meet OSPB standards, but sought to bring the facility up as much to the standards as possible, with a particular focus on mitigating the effects of an improvised explosive device (IED) attack on the compound. He stated:

In the specific case of Benghazi, we were aware that, you know, the villas they had rented would not meet. **Everybody was aware of it. Ambassador Stevens was aware of it.** The Department as a whole was aware that this did not meet standards. But what we did was put as much effort into it as we could to get as close as possible to the standards.

The most important consideration for Benghazi, the greatest threat that we were worried about -- well, there were two greatest threats that we were worried about. One is an attack on our vehicles when we are moving and the other is a car bomb or an IED of some sort. The reason we had -- we went into a villa complex in Benghazi that was of the size it was, was to

---

[104] Bultrowicz Tr. at 31-32.
[105] Boswell Tr. at 66.

give us the best possible standoff against an IED, which was the common form of attacking something in that part of the world.[106]

Nevertheless, Bultrowicz clarified that Benghazi was exempt from the waiver evaluation process because of the status granted it by Under Secretary Kennedy when he approved the one-year extension of the facility "as-is" in December 2011. He stated:

> A. I think in March, during one of these working groups, it was noted that there was authority to move into the facility as is but that a waiver packet would have to be done at a later date. But I don't think that packet was ever completed.
>
> Q. So was there, sort of, a directive not to do a waiver packet? Or who would have the authority to say, you can occupy this without doing a waiver packet?
>
> A. Well, not saying that anybody -- not saying that somebody said, "You don't have to do a waiver packet," but who could grant the authority to move into the building, I think that authority was given by the Under Secretary of Management, Mr. Kennedy.[107]

The Bureau of Near Eastern Affairs

The second State Department bureau that the ARB singled out for "systemic failures and leadership and management deficiencies" was the Near Eastern Affairs Bureau (NEA), a component of the Under Secretariat for Political Affairs. NEA is the chief policy-making bureau in the State Department with responsibility for the Middle East and North Africa, including Libya. While officials in NEA disagreed with this finding, some were aware of concerns about security but were unable to effectuate action to address those concerns.

Several senior officials within NEA told the Committee they disagreed with the ARB's findings with respect to their bureau, not least because NEA was not a bureau tasked with security functions prior to the Benghazi attack. For example, the Acting Assistant Secretary of Near Eastern Affairs, Ambassador Elizabeth Jones, a distinguished diplomat who holds the rank of Career Ambassador in the Senior Foreign Service, told the Committee she was unaware of the security problems at the Benghazi special mission compound. She also disagreed with the ARB's conclusions about her bureau. She stated:

> A. My reaction is that I wish I'd known what the situation there was. I wish I'd been told.
>
> Q. Do you believe there were leadership and management deficiencies

---

[106] *Id.* at 67-68 (emphasis added).
[107] Bultrowicz Tr. at 32.

within NEA?

A.   I do not.

Q. The finding refers to two bureaus at the State Department. Do you believe NEA to be one of those two bureaus?

A.   Yes, I do.[108]

Ambassador Jones and other senior officials who ran NEA told the Committee they had no responsibility for security policy and staffing in Libya, nor did they have the ability to affect those policies and staffing decisions. Rather, they maintained that this responsibility and authority rested entirely with the Diplomatic Security Bureau, a component of the Under Secretariat for Management. Ambassador Jones stated:

Q. What was NEA's role in security at U.S. embassies or U.S. facilities . . . in Libya?

A. The Near East Bureau has very little responsibility and capacity to determine security at embassies overseas. That responsibility at that time lay virtually entirely with the Diplomatic Security Bureau.[109]

Jones' deputy, Principal Deputy Assistant Secretary Elizabeth Dibble shared a similar sentiment with the Committee. She testified:

A.   I suppose that I would agree with the second part of the sentence, that the security posture was inadequate for Benghazi and was inadequate to deal with the attack. I would not necessarily agree that it was due to systematic failures in leadership and management deficiencies in the two bureaus at the State Department.
I think if you go down to the next paragraph of the report, it hits the -- you know, that's the nub of it, that things were stovepiped.

Q.   Uh-huh.

A.   But leadership and management deficiencies, I think, are broader than -- that is something different than stovepiping.[110]

Dibble also said:

If you're talking about the reporting chain, Lee Lohman did report to me, yes, and I reported to the assistant secretary. But security -- and again,

---

[108] Jones Tr. at 98.
[109] Jones Tr. at 12.
[110] Dibble Tr. at 87.

you know, this was pointed out in the report itself, decisions on security were stovepiped pre-Benghazi. And decisions on specific, you know, whether to put assets in Benghazi or in Bujumbura were made by the Bureau of Diplomatic Security, not by the regional bureaus. I mean, this is -- and this is sort of -- it's not just an NEA issue. It's across the board. The convention was that **regional bureaus did not have control over the security resources, control over the security people, and therefore control over security.**[111]

Lee Lohman, the head of the NEA Executive Office in charge of finance, personnel and general services support for the diplomatic mission in Libya, also shared his concerns about the ARB's finding with the Committee. He testified:

Q. Do you think that NEA had any significant role in the security posture of the special mission in Benghazi?

A. Let's go back to what we mean about the security posture again. We're talking about the number of agents on the ground, the training and composition of the guards, the fortification of the buildings, the security procedures that would be used to protect the facility. **There's no expertise in NEA that could competently provide an opinion on any of that. That's what we depended, relied on Diplomatic Security to provide.**[112]

Raymond Maxwell was the Deputy Assistant Secretary for Maghreb Affairs within NEA. U.S. foreign policy toward Libya fell within his portfolio. Maxwell was the only Department official within NEA whom the ARB held responsible for poor performance that contributed to the failures of Benghazi. Maxwell too shared a similar perspective with the Committee about NEA's relative lack of control over security resources and the security posture at the U.S. mission in Libya. He testified:

Q. What would be the role of Liz Dibble or Beth Jones in helping the folks who are in Libya make the case to management to get more security? I mean, certainly, if you were aware, if you were concerned, it's fair to say that Liz Dibble and Beth Jones were also aware, presumably concerned.

A. Yes.

Q. What would be their role in working with State Department management to help the security posture for the folks on the ground that were requesting it?

---

[111] *Id.* at 51 (emphasis added).
[112] Lohman Tr. at 34 (emphasis added).

A. It's typically a DS function, and so the DS Secretary would have the lead in this sort of cross-bureau environment, but it's certainly the case that...the NEA Assistant Secretary would advocate on behalf of posts to the DS Assistant Secretary.[113]

Notwithstanding Maxwell's statement that the NEA Assistant Secretary would advocate on behalf of her posts to the DS Assistant Secretary, Acting Assistant Secretary Jones told the Committee she did not do so with respect to the U.S. mission in Libya. Jones stated:

Q. And in your interactions, or I should say NEA's interactions with DS with . . . regard to security policy, did you have any direct interaction with your counterpart . . . Ambassador Boswell?

A. I had no interactions with Ambassador Boswell about security at Embassy Tripoli. . . . or at the [Benghazi] mission.[114]

Ambassador Jones' lack of awareness regarding security resourcing problems in Benghazi does not mean no one in NEA was aware of them. Since NEA serves as the chief interlocutor for U.S. ambassadors and their diplomatic officers in the region, it is not surprising that Ambassador Christopher Stevens and other members of his team routinely expressed their needs and concerns through NEA channels. These channels included either direct contact with the NEA front office via the Maghreb Desk, or through the NEA executive office (NEA/EX), which handled administrative matters such as human resources and finance for diplomatic missions in the region.[115] The needs and concerns expressed to NEA from the U.S. mission in Libya included DS's perennial understaffing of the Benghazi mission and a security environment that deteriorated rapidly in the summer of 2012.

For example, in February 2012, the U.S. principal officer stationed in Benghazi wrote to the NEA/EX desk officer in Washington:

For DS staffing, please let me know if there is anyone I can call. We had a short window yesterday when [the Information Management Officer] was alone without an RSO [Regional Security Officer] in the compound due to simultaneous movements by me and the TDYers [temporary duty DS officers]. We'll de-conflict so that does not happen again, but what that means, we will not be able to support any off-compound movements February 12 to 13. I will be restricted to a single movement at that time inside Benghazi city limits from February 14 to 24. We've heard that the agent scheduled to arrive February 13 is having visa issues. If he cannot travel as planned, we will be down to two agents from February 12 to 24 and restricted to compound.[116]

---

[113] Maxwell Tr. at 19.
[114] Jones Tr. at 23.
[115] Lohman Tr. at 8-9.
[116] State Department Production, Document No. C05389467 (Aug. 2013).

Lohman told the Committee he raised the shortage of DS agents in Benghazi with Charlene Lamb, the Deputy Assistant Secretary for International Programs in the Diplomatic Security Bureau. He stated:

> I said that we were concerned, because the implications of not having sufficient staffing in Benghazi . . . would have a direct operational impact, either . . . the [Information Management Officer], who was trying to protect the classified [communications equipment], would not have a regional security officer with him because they were out doing things, or the principal officer would not be able to get out to do his work. What could we do about this?[117]

As the Office Director for the Maghreb Office, William Roebuck was the executive officer to Deputy Assistant Secretary Raymond Maxwell and one of the most knowledgeable policy experts on Libya in the Department. Roebuck told the Committee that he was so concerned about the number of DS agents in Benghazi, he considered recommending to the number two in the Bureau, Elizabeth Dibble, that the post be shut down to "force the issue" with DS.

In an e-mail to a subordinate, Roebuck wrote: "I'm skeptical we will get anything more than minimal DS support (3). If it drops longer term to two DS agents, we should drop the caveats in the e-mail I will send to Liz [Dibble], and we should recommend closing [the Benghazi post] to force the issue. Nothing really to lose if we lose the argument."[118]

According to Roebuck, he never sent the proposed e-mail to Dibble, nor did he raise the issue of closing the Benghazi mission to "force the issue." He testified:

> Q.   What was the e-mail you were planning to send to Liz?
>
> A.   I don't know. There must have been something that Evyenia and I were drafting for Liz for her consideration, but I can't find a record of it, so I'm not --
>
> Q.   Okay. So you looked for a record of --
>
> A.   I did. This is one of the e-mails I had in my files, and I read it and looked, and I was unable to find anything.
>
> * * *
>
> Q.   What did you mean by closing? Closing the facility in Benghazi?
>
> A.   Yeah. That's what I was saying, yeah. As far as I can tell, I did not send such an e-mail, but it was -- that was definitely something

---

[117] Lohman Tr. at 126.
[118] State Department Production, Document No. C05395968 (Aug. 2013).

I was thinking about as a way to sort of force the issue.

Q.   Because of issues with DS staffing you were concerned about --

A.   Right.

Q.   -- the number of agents. Is that safe to say?

A. Right. Primarily because people out there were not able to do their
    work, they weren't able to move, they weren't able to do   the
    contact work that they wanted to do.[119]

* * *

Q.   [T]hat idea ... about closing, potentially closing Benghazi. Was
     that an idea that you discussed with anyone else?

A.   I don't have a recollection of discussing it. My sense of the e-mail
      is that I was, you know, gaming out some arguments about how to,
      you know, persuade people to provide additional security.[120]

NEA officials were aware of the difficulty the Benghazi post was having in receiving enough DS agents to protect the diplomats there and allow them to do their jobs. They were also aware of the significant deterioration in the security environment which began in the spring of 2012 with an attack on the compound itself and an assassination attempt on the British ambassador in Benghazi. For example, Roebuck told the Committee:

> There had been a substantial spike in violence. Most of it was Libyan-
> on-Libyan violence -- assassinations, abductions, some explosions,
> militia, inter-militia violence. But there had been the beginnings of some
> targeting of westerners. . . . And so I reached out to Chris [Stevens]. I
> said, you know, we're concerned about security for the people out there,
> and we should think about what we're doing with our staffing. And I see
> from his response he agreed.[121]

Roebuck told the Committee that, in response to the spike in violence in Benghazi, he delayed deploying a replacement principal officer to the compound:

A. And so [the outgoing principal officer] left, and I, as I remember, I
    delayed the arrival of the new principal officer for a period, as
    we sort of reassessed the situation out there . . . .

Q.   So do you recall sort of what that gap was or how long that space

---

[119] Roebuck Tr. at 81-82.
[120] *Id.* at 90.
[121] *Id.* at 87-88.

was where you held somebody back or didn't have somebody there?

A.   It was a few weeks, I think. It was about 3 weeks, 2 or 3 weeks.[122]

In short, at least some officials in NEA were aware of long-standing concerns at post that there were insufficient security resources in Benghazi. Yet, either they took no action to advocate for additional security resources to DS because they felt powerless to do so, or they did not raise these concerns with their NEA superiors who could take them to DS. As the ARB acknowledges, "security in Benghazi was not recognized and implemented as a 'shared responsibility' by the bureaus in Washington charged with supporting the post, resulting in stove-piped discussions and decisions on policy and security."[123] The ARB cited NEA for "systemic failures and leadership and management deficiencies," yet it singled out only one official for "accountability," an official whose failings were totally unrelated to the Benghazi tragedy – according to information obtained by the Committee.

Accountability Theater

On December 18, 2012—approximately ten weeks after it was convened—the ARB delivered a report that found certain senior State Department officials in Washington had "demonstrated a lack of proactive leadership and management ability appropriate for the State Department's senior ranks in their responses to security concerns posed by Special Mission Benghazi . . . ."[124] In the section entitled "Accountability of Personnel," the ARB report assigned blame to four State Department officials—Eric Boswell, Scott Bultrowicz, Charlene Lamb and Raymond Maxwell.[125] Within days, Secretary Clinton placed those four officials on administrative leave.

In December 2012, the Department's swift action against the individuals named in the ARB report fostered the perception that it had held individuals who were negligent in their responsibilities accountable. For example, a December 19, 2012 *New York Times* article stated:

> Four State Department officials were removed from their posts on Wednesday after an independent panel criticized the "grossly inadequate" security at a diplomatic compound in Benghazi, Libya, that was attacked on Sept. 11, leading to the deaths of Ambassador J. Christopher Stevens and three other Americans.[126]

---

[122] *Id.* at 88.
[123] ARB Report at 4.
[124] *Id.* at 39.
[125] *Id.*, Accountability section.
[126] Gordon & Schmitt, *supra* note 28.

The Administration also praised the State Department's swift action against the four individuals named in the ARB report. With reference to the four Department officials relieved of their duties based on the ARB's findings, White House Press Secretary Jay Carney said:

> [T]here has already been, in this very short period of time, actions that demonstrate accountability as being upheld . . . . Immediately, accountability has been brought to bear with regard to four individuals who are very senior.[127]

Documents and testimony obtained by the Committee give the impression that former Secretary Hillary Clinton's decision to announce action against the individuals named in the ARB report was more of a public relations strategy than a measured response to assign accountability where appropriate. Eight months later, in August 2013, Secretary Kerry reinstated the four officials placed on administrative leave. Secretary Kerry concluded that since they had not "breached their duties," none of the four should be fired, according to State Department spokesperson Marie Harf.[128]

On August 20, 2013, in a daily press briefing, Harf explained that the four officials were reinstated in part because taking adverse personnel action against them would serve merely to "make us all feel better." Harf stated:

> [W]e have to let the facts lead where they may, and these are people with real lives and real careers, and **we can't just take action that's not warranted against them just to make us all feel better**. That's not the way the process works, and quite frankly, we owe it more to our diplomats serving all around the world to have thorough processes and to look at all of this from an independent lens, which is exactly what the ARB did.[129]

Because the employees identified in the ARB report had not been negligent or willfully insubordinate, the ARB was not in a position to make recommendations regarding discipline. The State Department faced no such restrictions. Ambassador Pickering told the Committee that the Board felt that the actions of these individuals warranted discipline, but the ARB lacked the statutory authority to recommend specific disciplinary actions, absent a breach of duty. He stated:

> We were concerned that breach of duty had been defined, both in statute and regulation, in part through what are the normal processes of negotiation with labor unions and the State Department to the point where it required an element of extreme negligence and some element of willfulness. And the meaning of that, Mr. Chairman, is that you can't exercise what's called discipline, and the disciplines are three --

---

[127] The White House, Office of the Press Sec'y, Press Briefing by White House Press Sec'y Jay Carney (Dec. 20, 2012).

[128] Jay Solomon, *Kerry Reinstates Officials Suspended Over Benghazi Attack*, WALL ST. J., Aug. 21, 2013.

[129] Bureau of Public Affairs, U.S. Department of State, Daily press briefing, Statement of Deputy Spokesperson Marie Harf (Aug. 20, 2013) (emphasis added).

reprimand, suspension, and separation -- without finding the evidence sufficient to establish that. And we said, look, we did our best, but that was not there, but we found people so deficient in their performance of their duty that we felt that there should have been some discipline available.[130]

The ARB's limited authority—which does not extend to recommending adverse personnel action—is a weakness for which Congress may consider a legislative remedy. This limited authority is part of a larger concern about the ARB's evaluation of accountability related to the Benghazi attacks. Witnesses interviewed by the Committee raised questions about the ARB's findings regarding accountability, including whether individuals cited by the ARB actually had any responsibility for decisions related to security of U.S. facilities in Libya.

The fact that the ARB recommended discipline for four State Department officials who "demonstrated a lack of proactive leadership and management ability appropriate for the State Department's senior ranks in their responses to security concerns posed by Special Mission Benghazi," [131] and the fact that Secretary Kerry took eight months to rule out action against those four officials, calls into question the ARB's findings and the Department's faith in the work of the ARB.

More than one year since the attacks in Benghazi, and despite obvious failures by the State Department with regard to securing the Benghazi mission, no State Department official has been fired. No State Department official even missed a paycheck. Those most responsible for the attacks—the perpetrators—remain at large.

Raymond Maxwell's misconduct had no bearing on the security posture in Benghazi.

One of the four officials singled out by the ARB for accountability was Raymond Maxwell, the Deputy Assistant Secretary for Maghreb Affairs within NEA. Maxwell was the only individual within NEA criticized by the ARB. The criticism of Maxwell was included in a section of the classified version of the ARB report. That section was subsequently declassified. With regard to Maxwell, the ARB stated:

Mindful of the lesson that security is everyone's responsibility, Board members were troubled by the NEA DAS for Maghreb Affairs' lack of leadership and engagement on staffing and security issues in Benghazi. The Board was particularly concerned that an official at his senior level would make the affirmative decision not to read intelligence regularly when doing so might have given him a more informed understanding of the areas and issues under his responsibility, including security risks and needs. In contrast to the constant engagement by NEA Executive Office

---

[130] Pickering Tr. at 91-92.
[131] ARB Report at 39.

46

post management officers and the Office Director and staff for the Maghreb, the Maghreb DAS failed to provide tangible advocacy with DS in support of his subordinates' efforts and post's security requests.[132]

Maxwell was removed from his duties as Deputy Assistant Secretary for Maghreb Affairs on December 18, 2012, the same day the State Department released the unclassified version of the ARB report.[133] Three days later, Maxwell was notified that he had been placed on administrative leave.[134] As with the other three individuals placed on administrative leave, Maxwell was not fired—he continued to receive full salary and benefits. He was removed from his position and prohibited from performing any official duties for the Department.

The ARB's findings with respect to Maxwell are significant because he was the only official the ARB singled out for criticism within a bureau—NEA—which was found to suffer from "systemic failures and leadership and management deficiencies [which] resulted in a Special Mission security posture that was inadequate for Benghazi and grossly inadequate to deal with the attack that took place."[135] This finding is based entirely on Maxwell's conduct. In fact, Ambassador Pickering confirmed to the Committee that Maxwell's performance was the focus of this finding. He stated:

> Q. Were there systemic failures in leadership and management deficiencies within the NEA Bureau?
>
> A. Yes.
>
> Q. And what were they?
>
> A. The identification of Mr. Maxwell's failure fully to perform his duties as expected was the major identification that supported that judgment.
>
> Q. And were there any systemic failures in leadership and management deficiencies with any other officials in the NEA Bureau?
>
> A. No.[136]

An analysis of the ARB's critique of Maxwell's performance could reasonably be expected to shed light on the failures of NEA which led to Benghazi. In reality, however, the ARB's findings with respect to Maxwell raise more questions than answers.

---

[132] *Id.*, Accountability section.
[133] Maxwell Tr. at 28.
[134] *Id.* at 31.
[135] ARB Report, at 4.
[136] Pickering Tr. at 103-104.

According to NEA officials interviewed by the Committee, decisions about security policy and security resources rested firmly within the Bureau of Diplomatic Security, not NEA.[137] Therefore, the ARB's finding that Maxwell lacked "leadership and engagement on staffing and security issues in Benghazi" is puzzling. Maxwell himself denied having any formal role in determining the appropriate security posture or evaluating security requests by the U.S. mission in Libya. He testified:

> Q. And did you have any role in the security posture for Libya?
>
> A. No.
>
> * * *
>
> Q. Did you have any role in evaluating security requests for Libya, whether Tripoli or Benghazi?
>
> A. Technically, no. Those requests came in through the Executive Bureau, the Post Management Office. They were routed to the Executive Director who reports to PDAS, or they will also parallel-route it through Diplomatic Security and up through that chain of command.[138]

Similarly, the Principal Deputy Assistant Secretary in NEA, Elizabeth Dibble, told the Committee that Maxwell had no responsibility for security measures and should not have been held accountable by the ARB. She stated:

> Q. But, obviously, they did, you know, find Mr. Maxwell . . . culpable for something. I mean, do you feel that the finding with Mr. Maxwell speaks to a systemic failure of leadership and management deficiencies as it relates to security in Benghazi?
>
> A. No, because Mr. Maxwell wasn't -- in the context of the way the State Department, not just NEA but across the board, in which we were operating, you know, a year ago, the regional bureaus did not have oversight over implementation of security measures. And because of that, **I don't think he should be held responsible for what happened in Benghazi.**[139]

Lee Lohman, the Executive Director for NEA in charge of finance, personnel and general services issues for U.S. diplomatic facilities in Libya, agreed. He testified:

> A. For the people in Diplomatic Security, I didn't know what information the ARB had accumulated, I didn't know what their involvement on any specific decisionmaking might be, so . . . the

---

[137] Jones Tr. at 118.
[138] Maxwell Tr. at 14.
[139] Dibble Tr. at 88 (emphasis added).

justice of those decisions was something that I just had no idea about.

When I looked at Ray Maxwell's situation, I had a much better sense of how much he was or was not involved in this, and it struck me as being unfair.

Q.   Can you elaborate on that?

A. Well, he just wasn't involved in making decisions about the security of what was going on at post, because nobody in NEA was making those kind of detailed decisions.

Q.   **Was he making any decisions related to security at post**?

A.   **Not that I was aware of.**[140]

Testimony obtained by the Committee showed that concerns about the ARB's findings regarding Maxwell were not confined to his colleagues in NEA. Former Assistant Secretary for Diplomatic Security Eric Boswell—who was himself singled out by the ARB for management failures related to Benghazi—was also puzzled by the ARB's finding with respect to Maxwell's and the NEA Bureau's role in security. Boswell stated:

A.   I didn't see anything elsewhere in the report about systemic failure in the NEA Bureau. I'm sure they're talking about the NEA Bureau, but beyond saying that there was a DAS that they faulted, I didn't see any other --

Q.   That was Mr. Maxwell?

A.   Mr. Maxwell.

Q.   Were you surprised that Mr. Maxwell was in the accountability section, based upon your interaction with --

A.   I was a little surprised. I didn't know Mr. Maxwell.

Q.   Why were you surprised?

A.   I didn't know him as a player on the --

* * *

A.   I did not know Ray Maxwell, just didn't know him.

---

[140] Lohman Tr. at 115.

Q.   Didn't have any interaction with him?

A. Didn't have any interaction with him, had no reason to -- didn't understand why the ARB had mentioned him.[141]

The ARB's criticism of Maxwell focused on his "affirmative decision not to read intelligence regularly when doing so might have given him a more informed understanding of the areas and issues under his responsibility, including security risks and needs."[142] This finding represents the extent of the ARB's concerns about Maxwell's performance, which amounted to the entire basis for the ARB's finding that NEA suffered from "systemic failures and leadership and management deficiencies [which] resulted in a Special Mission security posture that was inadequate for Benghazi and grossly inadequate to deal with the attack that took place."[143] Pickering testified:

Q. Did the Board identify -- just sticking to Mr. Maxwell, did the Board identify any other concerns about Mr. Maxwell's performance that went beyond his failure to read the daily intelligence briefing materials?

A. **I believe we considered that sufficient unto itself.** And I don't want to take it any further without going back again and looking, but I think it's -- essentially that's the reason.[144]

Documents and testimony obtained by the Committee call into question the connection between Maxwell's performance and the security posture in Benghazi. It is unclear why the ARB based a significant finding—arguably the strongest one in the entire ARB Report—on Maxwell's failure to read daily intelligence briefings that did not bear on the security posture at U.S. diplomatic facilities in Benghazi. Several witnesses testified that Maxwell's decision to stop attending daily intelligence reviews had no bearing on what happened in Benghazi.

In July 2012, Maxwell stopped attending regular morning sessions where briefers from the Intelligence Community would make available daily "read-books" of intelligence reports relevant to the Bureau's area of operations.[145] At these read-book sessions, officials from the NEA front office would come at their convenience between about 7:30 am. and 9:00 a.m. to read through the daily intelligence reporting.[146] According to Maxwell, when the ARB interviewed him for a second time by the ARB, he informed the Board that he had stopped attending the read-book sessions in part because he found the intelligence to be of dubious value. Maxwell testified:

---

[141] Boswell Tr. at 120-21, 82.
[142] ARB Report, Accountability section.
[143] *Id.* at 4.
[144] Pickering Tr. at 149 (emphasis added).
[145] Maxwell Tr. at 66.
[146] Jones Tr. at 69-70.

Well, primarily because the intel was garbage. It was circular reporting. It was regurgitated Embassy reporting we were getting anyway. And what wasn't recirculated or regurgitated was spectacular and sensational and just not useful.[147]

Witnesses described the daily read books as "the funny book,"[148] or the "funny papers."[149]

Maxwell told the ARB that during the summer of 2012, he had been invited to give a number of public speeches and did not want to have trouble separating classified from unclassified information. He was trying to avoid inadvertently disclosing classified information in a public setting. He stated:

> I told them that part of my job included domestic outreach, and I had been to Nebraska, of all places, for a weekend of speaking engagements. I had been to Los Angeles and Santa Monica. I had briefed diplomatic delegations in Washington. I had done a series of briefings for Security Council member delegations who came down from New York. I talked to college students and think-tanks and a number of things, and I told them that I made a decision maybe July-August timeframe that I didn't need that spectacular sensationalism from the intel briefings from the morning readings bouncing around in my head during question-and-answer sessions with these briefings.[150]

According to Maxwell, what he failed to communicate to the ARB was that he did receive regular briefings on a number of classified programs and routinely read the cable traffic pertaining to his area of responsibility. He testified:

> Now, what they didn't give me a chance to say, and if they had checked I would have told them, that I was read into a couple of different programs that required compartmentalized information and special briefings, and when there was actionable intelligence, the analysts from INR [State Department Intelligence and Research Bureau] would call me, and I'd meet them in the SCIF, and he would make the information accessible to me, and that happened once every couple of weeks. Additionally, I read the cable traffic that came in every day through the classified open net.[151]

The ARB apparently interpreted Maxwell's comments about no longer attending the daily read-book sessions to mean he had stopped reading intelligence entirely. The ARB's senior leadership told the Committee that the Board believed Maxwell had stopped reading all intelligence materials. Admiral Michael Mullen, the ARB Vice-Chairman, stated:

---

[147] Maxwell Tr. at 25.
[148] *Id.* at 67.
[149] Dibble Tr. at 62.
[150] Maxwell Tr. at 25-26.
[151] *Id.* at 26.

Well, I think he indicated, I think he said publicly that he wasn't reading the intelligence. If you're going to -- it's just hard for me to understand how you could have any idea, particularly with respect to threat or potential or anything like that, that you're not paying attention to intelligence.[152]

Ambassador Pickering testified that he understood Maxwell's explanation that he stopped attending the daily intelligence sessions to mean that Maxwell had stopped reading all intelligence. Pickering testified:

A. I believe that his approach, which he described to us, his principal failing was that he made it apparently a practice not to read the intelligence.

Q. Okay. And specifically what type of intelligence do you recall him not reading?

A. **I took the statement to cover all intelligence**.

* * *

Q. Were there any other aspects of his performance that were lacking?

A. That was our principal concern.

Q. That he didn't read the intelligence generally or just the daily intelligence?

A. He said intelligence.[153]

Members of the ARB may have been confused as to what intelligence Maxwell was actually reading in the roughly two months prior to the Benghazi attacks. NEA officials interviewed by the Committee expressed concerns about how the ARB seized upon Maxwell's statement in its final report and linked his decision to skip the morning read-books sessions between July and September 2012 to the tragedy in Benghazi.

In an interview with the Committee, Maxwell's supervisor, Acting Assistant Secretary for NEA Elizabeth Jones, said that if she had known about Maxwell's decision to stop attending the daily read-book sessions, she would have insisted he do so.[154] However, she also unequivocally stated that there was no connection between Maxwell's decision with respect to the read-books and the loss of life in Benghazi. Jones testified:

---

[152] Mullen Tr. at 138.
[153] Pickering Tr. at 35-36 (emphasis added).
[154] Jones Tr. at 91.

Q. Do you believe that with respect to Ray Maxwell, do you believe that the -- do you believe what the Board found about Mr. Maxwell's conduct that it put in the report, was that at all related to a systemic failure or a leadership and management deficiency that was at all responsible for the security posture that was inadequate in Benghazi?

A. No. The issue that was reported about Ray in the ARB about his failure to read intelligence is a performance issue. **However, because it's been determined that there was no intelligence that could have told us that this attack was underway, it wasn't material.**[155]

Jones' deputy at NEA, Elizabeth Dibble, also felt it was inappropriate for Maxwell to stop attending the read-book sessions. [156] Still, like Jones, Dibble saw no connection between Maxwell not attending the read-book sessions and the security failures which contributed to the attacks in Benghazi. Dibble stated:

I don't think he was responsible for security in Libya, and so to be held accountable for security breaches, lapses, failures, however you want to characterize them, I don't think is right, for him to be held accountable, because he had no decision authority . . . he had no impact, no control over the allocation of security resources. . . . I am not sure that that is directly related to what happened in Benghazi because I don't see the link there, and I am not quite sure why the -- how the ARB, I mean, if he said some of these things, it does strike me as odd and off and not what one would expect from a senior officer. But, again, that's not -- it doesn't fall into lack of -- you know, dereliction of duty or anything with regard to Benghazi.[157]

Despite focusing on Maxwell's actions with respect to intelligence and drawing a connection between those actions and the security situation in Benghazi, the ARB did not ask key witnesses any questions about that issue. Maxwell's supervisor and colleagues could have provided context for Maxwell's testimony to the Board before it held him accountable for actions the Board found to have contributed to the inadequate security posture in Benghazi. The ARB did not ask them. Maxwell's direct supervisor, Acting Assistant Secretary for NEA Elizabeth Jones, was interviewed twice by the ARB. She told the Committee the ARB never asked her about Maxwell's conduct or performance. Ambassador Jones testified:

Q. [A]t neither meeting were you asked about your supervision of Mr. Maxwell. Is that correct?

---

[155] *Id.* at 98-99
[156] Dibble Tr. at 64.
[157] Dibble Tr. at 64-65.

A.   I believe that to be the case.   I don't recall any question
       about personnel issues.[158]

                                    * * *

Q.   Would you have preferred that, as Mr. Maxwell's supervisor, [the
       ARB] had consulted you about his performance matter issues?

A.   Yes, because I could have told them that he had planned to retire
       within 3 days of the Benghazi attack happening.

Q.   Why is that relevant?

A.   I believe it's potentially, possibly relevant as to why Ray Maxwell
       stopped reading intelligence.

Q.   Could you elaborate on it?

A.   He told me, when I talked to him about it, that he had stopped
       reading intelligence in the weeks before he retired so he wouldn't
       get mixed up in public statements about what was classified and
       what was unclassified, about what he knew about the countries in
       his region.

Q.   Did you find that to be a sensible reason?

A.   No, because I think it's quite easy to keep separate.

Q.   Did you tell him that at the time?

A.   I did.

Q.   What did he say?

A.   He didn't say anything. But I was more concerned that he had not
       given that explanation to the ARB, because I thought that that
       would have given better context to the statement that he made to
       the ARB.

Q.   And just to be clear, what was your understanding of the statement
       that he made to the ARB?

A.   That he had stopped reading intelligence in the weeks before the
       attack.[159]

_____

[158] Jones Tr. at 99.
[159] Jones Tr. at 100-101

The ARB's approach to assigning accountability within NEA for the failures that led to the Benghazi tragedy is puzzling. The ARB identified "systemic failures and leadership and management deficiencies at senior levels" within NEA. It seems obvious that a "systemic failure" within a large organization such as NEA could only result from a widespread failure throughout the system, either to recognize the challenges posed by the inadequate security posture of the Benghazi mission in a deteriorating environment, or else to take the appropriate steps to rectify it in order to safeguard American lives. Yet within the entire NEA Bureau, the ARB singled out only Raymond Maxwell, for conduct his own supervisor contended was not "material" to what happened in Benghazi.

If Ambassador Jones and others are right, and the intelligence Maxwell stopped reading was not material because NEA was essentially powerless to affect the actions of DS in Benghazi, it is unclear why the ARB blamed Maxwell for not reading it. If the intelligence did provide some kind of insight which could have prevented the failures of Benghazi, it is further unclear why Maxwell was held accountable for not reading it, but Ambassador Jones and others within NEA were not held accountable for having read it and taken no effective steps to remedy the shortcomings of the Benghazi compound's security posture before it led to a loss of life?

The ARB appropriately criticized Charlene Lamb's actions but downplayed how the Under Secretary for Management influenced her decisions.

The ARB leveled specific criticism at Charlene Lamb, the Deputy Assistant Secretary for International Programs, for the Diplomatic Security Bureau's failure to provide the full complement of five special agents for Benghazi. DAS Lamb repeatedly sought to limit the number of agents in Benghazi. She also ignored her subordinates' efforts to improve staffing levels. Still, the temporary nature of the facility provides important context for her actions. Under Secretary Kennedy, her superior, approved that decision.

Lamb remained consistently resistant to providing the five DS special agents earmarked for the Benghazi special mission compound by the December 2011 memorandum signed by Under Secretary Kennedy. The DS desk officer for Libya told the Committee:

> The RSO in Tripoli, the primary RSO, he was -- you know, he wanted his
> five agents which he thought was due to him from the memorandum that
> was signed on December 27th. Several different issues impacted on the --
> particularly in that timeframe. We already spoke about the trouble we
> were having getting TDY personnel. At that time I was still attempting to
> get five agents for most of that period?
>
> In mid-February, in conversations with DAS Lamb, it became quite -- she
> made it quite apparent that she wanted **three agents on the ground in
> Benghazi**. From that time on, I was attempting to get three agents into

Benghazi at all times.[160]

According to individuals interviewed by the Committee, Lamb's resisted staffing Benghazi to the full complement of DS agents because she believed that DS special agents had been poorly utilized in Benghazi. One of her principle concerns was the reliance of DS agents to drive the special mission compound's armored vehicles, a role typically fulfilled by locally employed staff in other countries.[161]

Lamb's resistance to providing more DS special agents continued even after an apparent terrorist IED attack on the Benghazi compound on June 6, 2012, which blew a hole in the perimeter wall. At that time, the RSO in Tripoli renewed his request for the full complement of five DS agents for Benghazi. Both Lamb's Regional Director for Near Eastern Affairs as well as the Libya desk officer strongly supported this request. The desk officer told the Committee:

Q. Based on your experience, just from a personal perspective, did you support that number or support that assessment?

A. Yes. Not only did I support it, I sent it to the RSO for clearance as well, which he supported fully, and I drafted an action memorandum stating the RSO's request.

Q. And what happened to that action memorandum?

A. It was approved by my direct supervisors, and then it was upstairs for a while. And we didn't hear anything. We felt it urgent enough, my supervisor scheduled a meeting with DAS Lamb, and in the meeting with DAS Lamb, essentially the long and short of it, the memo was denied for additional resources, personnel-wise.[162]

* * *

I mean, by the memo, I thought it was pretty clear. I had outlined the anti-Western attacks. My feelings, along with the RSO's -- and both RSOs opposed, and my superiors, we tried to advocate for additional security resources. It was denied. It wasn't outright denied. It was -- she wanted to know specifically what programs that the additional agents would be working on.[163]

Lamb also seemed very resistant to continuing the mission of the Department of Defense (DOD) Security Support Team (SST), a cadre of 16 special operators seconded to the State Department and placed under the authority of the Chief of Mission. DOD provided the team to State on a cost reimbursable basis, meaning the only costs to the State Department to have it in

---

[160] Papanu Tr. at 23.
[161] See id. at 58.
[162] Id. at 42-43.
[163] Id. at 44.

Libya were for transport, room and board. The SST deployed to Libya on 120-day deployments, which had to be renewed periodically in order to keep the team there. Although a handful of SST members were sent to Benghazi on a number of occasions to reinforce security there, the SST was primarily a Tripoli-based security asset.

In Tripoli, the SST provided critical protection for the visits of numerous U.S.-based personnel to Libya as part of the Administration's plans to assist the new Libyan government. According to William Roebuck, Director of the Maghreb Office within NEA:

> A. The NSS [National Security Staff], like a number of people in the interagency, wanted to get more assistance to the Libyan government on a range of areas, democracy in government, helping them rebuild their security institutions, helping with civil society. And the way that we were structured to do that was to send out TDYers to do it for a few weeks at a time, and that was difficult, because the embassy was just getting stood up again; they had limited bed space and other ability to support these visits, so they were pushing back, and so there was some friction between post and interagency about, you know, how to properly manage that desire to get assistance out to the Libyan government.

> * * *

> Q. Was the DOD SST presence . . . necessary to ensure that the staffing that was being pushed by NSS, the numbers, the individuals being pressed had adequate security to be able to get out and, you know, fulfill the responsibilities that they were being asked to do?

> A. I think the SST team was an important part of that security. I mean, they were a vital component in it. DS also provided regular RSO, ARSO folks and MSD teams. And all that together provided the security for the embassy and the security for TDYers, movements, et cetera. And, yeah, that kind of -- taken together, all that security support was essential to allow the embassy to function and to allow the TD wires to get out there and to provide assistance to the Libyans.[164]

As early as February, Lamb had been pushing to end the SST mission, despite strenuous objections from the Embassy in Tripoli. The Committee asked the Libya desk officer in DS about this. Papanu stated:

> Q. I will just read it for the record. So it is an e-mail from you on Friday, February 3rd, 2012. It is unclassified. It looks like it is to Eric Nordstrom and CC Jim Bacigalupo and Daniel Meehan. The

---

[164] Transcribed Interview of William Roebuck, Transcript at 120-22 (Aug. 5, 2013) [hereinafter Roebuck Tr.].

subject is "DS/IP meeting on Tripoli." So you wrote, "Eric, we had a meeting with DAS Lamb and DS/IP/OPO yesterday on Tripoli. Here are a couple of takeaways. One, DS/IP is not going to support extension of the DOD SST team past April 5. Please start thinking about what post could potentially need from DOS assets (high threat trained agents and SPS were both mentioned)."

* * *

A. [O]ne of the things that DAS Lamb mentioned in this meeting, obviously, was she was not going to support the extension of the DOD/SST team.[165]

The Ambassador and his staff in Tripoli at the time were taken aback by Lamb's position. In an e-mail, Ambassador Gene Cretz—Chris Stevens' immediate predecessor—wrote:

I fail to see the logic as to why DS would not support an extension of SST, unless DOD is against it which we have no inkling of . . . . The bottom line is we will be severely impacted without them and no one here is arguing that there has been any improvement in the security situation which would argue that they are no longer needed.[166]

The Ambassador's deputy weighed in as well, saying that "This is an untenable position."[167]

Although SST was extended past April 5, it would prove to be the final extension of the team's mission. In July 2012, Under Secretary Kennedy informed DOD that the State Department would not be requesting a further extension of the SST mission. A handful of DOD special operators remained in Tripoli past the early August expiration date of the SST to provide training for their Libyan military counterparts. According to Roebuck, Ambassador Stevens and his colleagues at the Embassy would have preferred to keep the SST running, in part to provide security. Roebuck stated:

Q. And your sense at the time was that post did want to extend the group? Or were they more focused on shifting the mission of the group?

A. They wanted to extend it for a substantial period. At a certain point, I think they realized -- and this was later than this memo. It would have been -- you know, later in the summer, they realized that, you know, changing -- in fact, in here, it is already evident that changing the nature of the mission was a good way to ensure that at least some of the people stayed on the ground and would

---

[165] Papanu Tr. at 97-98.

[166] E-mail from Gene A. Cretz to Elizabth L. Dibble, "FW: DS/IP meeting notes on Tripoli" (Feb. 14, 2012, 3:41 a.m.).

[167] E-mail from Joan Polaschik to Gene A. Cretz, "RE: DS/IP meeting notes on Tripoli" (Feb. 14, 2012, 7:53 a m.).

help provide some security at post. And then they wanted this -- also, post was strongly supportive of this [training] mission. So keeping people on the ground also supported that mission.

Q. But part of the motivation, at least as you understood it, was to have those assets on the ground from a security perspective as much as a training program?

A. I think so, yeah. Simply because they were -- they had been part of the security team. You know, they were armed and trained. And even if they were focused primarily on the training of Libyan CT forces, they could be an asset to help post. I think that was the thinking of Chris.

* * *

I mean, Chris' general predisposition was to keep the SST guys out there.

Q. From a training or a security standpoint? Or for both?

A. The predisposition I am talking about is for security. But I think he also recognized as the mission for -- at least a piece of the SST change that it would -- you know, it would be a good asset to provide the [counterterrorism] training but also to provide some security for post and be a rationale for keeping some of those guys at post.

Q. Was there a concern about security if the SST team left, that the post would lack the adequate security resources?

A. I think that is probably -- yeah. I think that is a fair description based on what I have seen from, you know, RSO e-mails and indications from Chris.[168]

These examples, and others described to the Committee in documents and testimony, suggest that the ARB's citation of Lamb's poor management was certainly justified. Nonetheless, the ARB downplayed the effect of decisions made by Lamb's superiors that contributed to her actions. Lamb failed to heed the recommendations of both the RSO in Tripoli and her subordinates in Washington to increase the number of DS agents in Benghazi in the wake of the June 6, 2012 terrorist attack on the compound. As mentioned earlier, Lamb's office was struggling to provide enough TDY DS agents to the mission in Libya in part because the temporary nature of those missions had forced them to use a personnel system to supply those agents which was never designed to handle the workload. The temporary, ad hoc nature of the mission in Libya was not a decision made at Lamb's level, or indeed even within the DS bureau.

---

[168] Roebuck Tr. at 127-129.

Rather, the Department's top leadership made this decision. And while Lamb's resistance to extending the SST mission, particularly as early as February 2012, is difficult to understand, the fact remains that the ultimate decision to end that mission rested with, and was taken by, Under Secretary Kennedy.[169]

It is unclear why the ARB did not hold the Under Secretary for Management accountable for decisions that affected the security posture in Benghazi.

The ARB correctly identified a number of failures which contributed to the Benghazi tragedy, however; the Board stopped short of identifying the root causes of those failures. In particular, the ARB appeared remarkably uncurious about the role of decisions made by officials above the four identified by the ARB as "accountable" for the failures of Benghazi. Witnesses questioned the ARB's reluctance to examine the effects of decisions made at more senior levels within the State Department.

Gregory Hicks, the former Deputy Chief of Mission at Embassy Tripoli, told the Committee that the ARB, in his view, may have overlooked the extensive role of Under Secretary for Management Patrick Kennedy in the relevant Benghazi-related decision making. Hicks testified:

> In our system, people who make decisions have been confirmed by the Senate to make decisions. The three people in the State Department who are on administrative leave pending disciplinary action are below Senate confirmation level. Now, the DS assistant secretary resigned, and he is at Senate confirmation level. Yet the paper trail is pretty clear that decisions were being made above his level. Certainly the fact that Under Secretary Kennedy required a daily report of the personnel in country and who personally approved every official American who went to Tripoli or Benghazi, either on assignment or TDY, would suggest some responsibility about security levels within the country lies on his desk. So, you know -- and since DS works for him as well and therefore threat reporting should be coming up to him, and so, you know, the ability -- at his point, it is pretty clear that personnel and threat meet. Not only that, but budget also meets at his desk, so, you know, if we assume that in our system, Senate confirmation means you get to make decisions, the under secretary for management is confirmed by the Senate, his appointment.[170]

As previously discussed, the decision by Ambassador Kennedy to approve the extension of the Benghazi special mission compound for one year as a temporary, residential facility had a number of negative effects on the U.S. Government's ability to provide adequate personnel and

---

[169] Bultrowicz Tr. at 132.
[170] Transcribed Interview of Gregory Hicks by H. Comm. on Oversight and Gov't Reform Comm. staff, Transcript at 115-166 (Apr. 11, 2013).

physical security resources. The former Assistant Secretary for Diplomatic Security, Eric Boswell, confirmed that Kennedy approved this extension. He testified:

> Q. Did you feel that there were any decisions related to security in Libya that involved individuals above you in the chain of command?

> A. Involving security in Libya, yes. The Under Secretary for Management was definitely involved in decisions involving -- lots of decisions about Benghazi. He's the one, after all, that authorized, gave the go-ahead for the mission in the first place and extended the mission. He approved the extension of the temporary mission.[171]

* * *

> Q. You said the memo that went to Under Secretary Kennedy, though?

> A. Right, right. The December whatever it was memo that went -- to which I referred earlier, the decision memo regarding extending the temporary facility in Benghazi.

> Q. Does that mean it was the Under Secretary of Management's decision that it be a temporary facility?

> A. Yes, yes. It was certainly his decision to authorize the extension, so, yes,[172]

Similarly, the decision to end the SST mission in Libya in July 2012 was made by Ambassador Kennedy, albeit based upon a recommendation from Charlene Lamb. Assistant Secretary for DS Eric Boswell testified:

> Q. Who were the decisionmakers relative to the -- either the presence or the mission of the SST?

> A. The ultimate decisionmaker is Under Secretary Kennedy.[173]

Scott Bultrowicz—Boswell's deputy—agreed. He stated:

> Well, again, he was certainly involved in the discussion whether or not the SST was going to be extended, because I think DOD reached out actually directly to Under Secretary Kennedy on that.[174]

---

[171] Boswell Tr. at 92.
[172] *Id.* at 29-30.
[173] *Id.* at 125.

The Committee interviewed several State Department officials who testfied that Ambassador Kennedy was very involved in other aspects of the U.S. diplomatic mission in Libya, including the Benghazi special mission compound. Ambassador Boswell gave testimony that is consistent with testimony provided at the Committee's May 8, 2013 hearing. He told the Committee that Ambassador Kennedy was involved in staffing and budgets for Libya. He testified:

Q.   And this is maybe a bit repetitive of what we just talked about, but at the May 8th hearing this committee held, a number of the witnesses raised questions about Under Secretary Kennedy's role in decisions related to Libya. They suggested that he was very involved in decisions related to staffing and budget. Do you agree or disagree with that?

A.   I do agree. He was very aware of what was going on in Libya and was involved in decisions. Sure, I agree with that. [175]

* * *

Q.   Beyond him approving the extension, was he involved in any other discussions about Libya or decisions related to Libya?

A.   That I am aware of -- you have to understand that Libya was -- Tripoli and Benghazi were unaccompanied posts. It is the Department's policy and practice to handle unaccompanied posts in a particular way. Unaccompanied, I mean with no families. And so any decision about travel in and out, staffing levels was made by the Under Secretary for Management.

Q.   Is that staffing of security and political staff?

A.   All, all, all positions.

Q.   So any decisions on staffing would --

A.   Staff size, yes. He would personally approve them.

Q.   Okay. And you wouldn't be involved in the discussion?

A.   DS might be involved with his staff, I might be involved, yes. [176]

---

[174] Bultrowicz Tr. at 132.
[175] Boswell Tr. at 93-94.
[176] Boswell Tr. at 92.

Deputy Assistant Secretary for Maghreb Affairs Raymond Maxwell also told the Committee that Ambassador Kennedy was intimately involved in the details for Libya. Maxwell testified:

> Q. The DCM, Mr. Hicks, testified that Ambassador Kennedy was very engaged on a minute level about the incidents that were occurring in Benghazi in the months leading up to the attacks.
>
> A. Yep.
>
> Q. Does that surprise you?
>
> A. It does not. We--one of the things that I found interesting was that the Under Secretary approved every person that went in or came out of Tripoli. Now, that's the Under Secretary . . . . [T]here were times when the Under Secretary for Management would delegate that authority to the Assistant Secretary of the regional bureau affected or to the Ambassador at post. But Pat Kennedy has never done that.[177]
>
>   * * *
>
> A. The DAS Assistant Secretary reports to the Under Secretary for Management. **The way the Under Secretary for Management runs things, there is no decision that DS makes that doesn't have his input and his imprimatur, his approval. There is no decision that DS doesn't make that doesn't have his disapproval.** DS--the Under Secretary for Management speaks for DS for all practical purposes, and there is no decision that DS makes that the Under Secretary for Management is not involved in.
>
> Q. **So, the important decisions about the security posture in Libya leading up to the attacks, if Mr. Boswell was held accountable for those decisions, is it fair to say that the Under Secretary for Management would have had a role in those decisions?**
>
> A. **Absolutely.**[178]

Lee Lohman, the Executive Director of the Near Eastern Affairs Bureau, told the Committee that Kennedy was personally involved in reviewing the schematics of the villas to be occupied by the U.S. diplomats in Benghazi. He stated:

> A. I was at least in one meeting where the undersecretary himself was looking at the -- the schematics and looking at which property would be selected and so on and offering opinions, but the staffers

---

[177] Maxwell Tr. at 87-88.
[178] *Id.* at 87.

were . . . constantly providing input to us; not in . . . the sense of them having a personal opinion, but they were conveying the wishes of the undersecretary.

Q.   Is that a normal arrangement . . . for M to be involved in selecting the facilities?

A.   When you say, 'normal,' what do you mean?

Q.   Is that common for the State Department?

A.   In a situation like this, it's . . . consistent with . . . past practice for the undersecretary to be involved.

Q.   Past practice throughout your experience . . . at the State Department?

A.   Well, I think it . . . depends on the undersecretary. Some . . . get more into the detail than others.

Q. I guess we have heard that Undersecretary Kennedy is very involved . . . in the details. Would you say he was more involved in the details on this . . . decision than --

A.   Yes.

* * *

Q.   So Undersecretary Kennedy and his staff conveying his desires was heavily involved in that discussion?

A.   Heavily.[179]

According to Acting Assistant Secretary for NEA, Ambassador Elizabeth Jones, before the Benghazi attack, any disagreements between her Bureau and the Diplomatic Security Bureau would be adjudicated by Pat Kennedy. Jones testified:

[I]f there was a disagreement between the Near East Bureau and Diplomatic Secretary, how would that be adjudicated or how -- to whom would we -- it would go to Under Secretary Pat Kennedy.[180]

Documents and testimony show that Ambassador Kennedy attended regular meetings with DS and NEA where, among other subjects, Libya was a topic of discussion. For example,

---

[179] Lohman Tr. at 26-27.
[180] Jones Tr. at 34-35.

Brian Papanu, the DS desk officer for Libya, described a July 2, 2012 meeting where the future of the Benghazi special mission compound beyond December 2012 was discussed. He stated:

> Q.   Do you recall the . . . July 2nd meeting with Under Secretary Kennedy?
>
> A.   I do.
>
> Q.   Did you attend that meeting?
>
> A.   I did.
>
> Q.   Can you provide us your recollection of that meeting?
>
> A. Certainly . . . From my recollection, the only Libya mention was a question NEA -- I believe it was NEA/EX, but it could have been NEA/MAG -- about the continued presence in Benghazi.
>
> Q.   And . . . what was the question posed to him?
>
> A.   Essentially, I can't remember the specifics, but are we going to continue with the mission in Benghazi.
>
> Q.   And was Under Secretary Kennedy present at the meeting?
>
> A.   He was.
>
> Q.   And do you recall what his response was?
>
> A.   His response was he had to check with S.
>
> Q.   And by 'S,' what does that mean?
>
> A.   That would be Secretary of State.[181]

To date, it is unclear whether Ambassador Kennedy ever discussed this matter with Secretary of State Hillary Clinton. The role of senior State Department leadership other than Kennedy in determining the parameters of Benghazi as an *ad hoc*, temporary mission remains one of the many questions the Committee intends to answer through its ongoing investigation.

E-mails reviewed by the Committee, however, show it is likely that Secretary Clinton's views played some role in the decision making on the future of the U.S. diplomatic mission in Benghazi. For example, in September 2011, when the Department was discussing what to do with the Benghazi special mission compound in the wake of the reopening of the U.S. Embassy in Tripoli, several NEA officials discussed the Secretary's desire to continue operating the

---

[181] Papanu Tr. 115-116.

Benghazi mission. Lee Lohman wrote: "Do I remember correctly that the Secretary had views about keeping Benghazi going?"[182]

Another State Department official responded: "Not sure. [A]long the lines of what Chris [Stevens] has laid out, i.e., for another six months or so? I am not sure if she had views of anything longer term than that."[183]

Raymond Maxwell replied:

> I remember [Assistant Secretary of NEA] Jeff [Feltman] (or somebody very important) saying that S definitely wanted Benghazi to continue operations for some time to come. No specifics were mentioned though.[184]

Elizabeth Dibble responded. She wrote:

> I raised with [NEA Assistant Secretary Jeffrey Feltman]. He thinks Chris needs to stay in Benghazi until [REDACTED] has relocated more or less permanently to Tripoli. He also thinks we should not rush to shut down operation there; this is in keeping with what the Secretary has said.[185]

The ARB downplayed the importance of the decisions made above DS and NEA. Documents and witness testimony show that these decisions—including those made by the Under Secretary for Management and other senior State Department officials—influenced or informed the actions of those under their supervision. The importance of such decisions will be a continued focus of the Committee's investigation.

In the rush to assign blame for the events leading up to the attacks in Benghazi, the State Department accepted the ARB findings regarding accountability at face value and immediately placed the careers of four public servants into bureaucratic purgatory.

There is no question that any individual whose actions contributed to the inadequate security posture in Benghazi should be held accountable. The ARB took this responsibility seriously and went above and beyond their predecessors in assigning accountability to four State Department officials. Documents and testimony, however, have raised questions about the adequacy of the ARB's findings with respect to accountability, and whether State Department leadership relied on the ARB's recommendations regarding accountability in the absence of doing their own evaluation of officials above the Assistant Secretary level. The Committee's investigation will continue to focus on identifying all the State Department officials who bore responsibility for the inadequate security posture in Benghazi.

---

[182] State Department Production, Document No. C05389443 (Aug. 2013).

[183] *Id.*

[184] *Id.*

[185] *Id.*

U.S. Diplomacy in Libya: Expeditionary or Expedient?

Another consequence of the ARB downplaying decisions made above the Assistant Secretary level in assigning accountability for the failures of Benghazi may be that the ARB missed the larger context of the Benghazi tragedy, namely the State Department's decision to operate the U.S. diplomatic presence in Libya as an *ad hoc* and poorly-defended outpost of what the Department has labeled "expeditionary diplomacy." As a result, the State Department may not learn all the right lessons from the Benghazi tragedy. In particular, the Department may need to figure out how to strike a better balance between the perceived policy imperative of operating in a particular location and the exigencies of operating in dangerous and unstable environments without adequate U.S. or host nation security support.

The Committee heard different views about what expeditionary diplomacy actually means; however, witnesses consistently testified that it involves operating diplomatic outposts in unstable environments which, in the past, the State Department believed were too dangerous to host diplomats. According to Principal Deputy Assistant Secretary for Near Eastern Affairs Elizabeth Dibble, the ARB failed to grasp the significance of the role played by expeditionary diplomacy in its analysis of the Benghazi tragedy. Dibble testified:

A.   There were parts of [the ARB report] that I felt perhaps missed the larger context in which we are operating now.

Q.   Can you elaborate on that?

A.   Things changed in the way we conduct our diplomacy in the period after Iraq, and we are now operating in places where 15 years ago we would have been pulling people out. Instead we are putting people in. And the phrase 'expeditionary diplomacy' really does mean something. And at least in the Near East world, things have gotten much harder and, frankly, much more dangerous. You know, 30 years ago Beirut was the anomaly, it was the exception, and now we have more posts that are under some sort of restriction -- or we're probably 50-50 now. But even Cairo, which had always been our big -- you know, it was the center of the -- the beating heart of the Arab world, as they say, is now on ordered departure. Tunisia, where I served, is an unaccompanied post.

So things have changed. And what I wasn't sure came through in the report was how much things have changed since Iraq and how we as foreign service officers are being asked to operate in a different context and world than we were certainly when I joined.[186]

---

[186] Dibble Tr. at 72-73.

According to former Assistant Secretary for Diplomatic Security Eric Boswell, expeditionary diplomacy involves the Department operating in "war zones," often alongside the U.S. Armed Forces. Boswell stated:

> It's the central policy question that we have to deal with in DS, and the Department for that matter. I think I have very good perspective … with which to answer that question because I have been Assistant Secretary twice, the last time in the '90s, before the term "expeditionary diplomacy" ever was coined. It was in 2003, in the wake of 9/11, the 9/11/2001, that -- that the United States Government made a decision that it would operate embassies in places where in my previous incarnation we never would have been, specifically war zones, war zones where there is active combat, and U.S. troops for that matter.[187]

Former Director of the Diplomatic Security Service Scott Bultrowicz believed expeditionary diplomacy certainly involved danger, and sometimes involved U.S. diplomats operating out of *ad hoc* physical facilities. Bultrowicz stated:

> [W]hen you talk about expeditionary diplomacy and you talk about deploying to these types of places, there has to be a recognition that there is a threat that it could happen, especially if you're not going into a purpose-built facility where you have all of the resources and manpower that you do in Kabul or Iraq.[188]

However, unlike Iraq and Afghanistan, where the Department has relied heavily on the U.S. military (and now on a small army of armed private security contractors in Iraq) to provide a strong outer defense for its facilities, U.S. diplomats in Libya were forced to operate in a dangerous and unstable environment without reliable U.S. or host nation security support. Lee Lohman, the Executive Director of the Near Eastern Affairs Bureau, testified:

> [R]emember that Benghazi, I'm not sure that we -- I'm trying to think back. I mean, we've evacuated from any number of places, but I'm not sure we've ever gone into something in such an expeditionary way as this by ourselves without having military along with us.[189]

Brian Papanu, the DS desk officer for Libya, told the Committee that host nation security support had been better in the war-torn nation of Liberia than in Benghazi. He testified:

> A. Well, Benghazi was definitely unique in almost every -- I can't think of a mission similar to this ever, and definitely in recent history. Potentially the closest I can think of was when we went into Monrovia, but there we had pretty decent host nation support, as far as I know.

---

[187] Boswell Tr. at 112.
[188] Bultrowicz Tr. at 139.
[189] Lohman Tr. at 106.

Q.   I am sorry, so Liberia had better host nation support than Benghazi?

A.   That was my understanding.[190]

Former Deputy Chief of Mission in Libya, Greg Hicks, told the Committee that because the mission in Libya was part of the Department's expeditionary diplomacy approach, he and his colleagues had to make do with fewer security resources than were needed. He stated:

> [Y]ou know, this was expeditionary diplomacy…we were doing our best with the resources that we had . . . when we got there, we arrived in Libya, we didn't have the security resources that we needed[191]

Documents and testimony obtained by the Committee during the course of its investigation show that the *ad hoc* facility in Benghazi, rather than being an example of expeditionary diplomacy, was instead an expedient way to maintain a diplomatic presence in a dangerous place. The State Department was operating a temporary residential facility in a violent and unstable environment without adequate U.S. and host nation security support.

The ARB recognized that in Benghazi the Department failed to strike "the proper balance between acceptable risk and expected outcomes in high risk, high threat areas."[192] Because the decision to keep the Benghazi mission running in the face of a dangerous environment without adequate U.S. or host nation security support was made at a level above which the ARB decided to assign accountability, it is unclear whether the ARB's report will result in a Department better able to strike the appropriate balance in the future.

The State Department Eagerly Relied on the Flawed Accountability Findings in the ARB Report

The ARB released its unclassified report on December 18, 2012. The classified version of the report identified four State Department officials whose actions, in the ARB's opinion, contributed to the inadequate security posture in Benghazi. It did not, however, find that the conduct of any of these officials constituted a "breach of duty." Absent this statutorily defined standard, the Board lacked the authority to effect any specific personnel actions. The ARB instead took the unprecedented step of issuing findings for individuals who they believed bore some responsibility for the inadequate security posture in Benghazi. In addition, they provided recommendations for administrative, not disciplinary, action against two of these individuals. In doing so, the Board circumvented the limitations of the existing statute and left it up to the State Department to act on these findings and recommendations.

---

[190] Papanu Tr. at 96-97.
[191] Hicks Tr. at 101.
[192] ARB Report at 8.

State Department leadership accepted the ARB's personnel findings and acted immediately to create the appearance of accountability.

The Department accepted the ARB's findings and recommendations regarding accountability without delay. Shortly after the report was delivered to the Secretary, the four officials cited by the ARB were relieved of their duties. Within days, all four were "placed on administrative leave pending further review."[193] As discussed above, the focus on these four individuals raises as many questions as answers.

Witnesses testified that the decision to act on the ARB's findings came from the very top of the Department. Raymond Maxwell, the Deputy Assistant Secretary for Maghreb Affairs within NEA, was one of the four individuals cited by the ARB. The day that the ARB report was released, Ambassador Elizabeth Jones, the Assistant Secretary for NEA, summoned Maxwell to her office. Jones informed him that Secretary Clinton had decided to relieve Maxwell of his duties. He testified:

> I went to the office, Beth closed the door. She said, 'Ray, the ARB Report was released today.' She said, 'It was not complimentary to the Department, it was not complimentary to the NEA Bureau, and it was not complimentary to you.' She said, 'In fact, it was so uncomplimentary to you that I have been told by Cheryl Mills to relieve you of your DAS position, to fire you.' She said, 'So, you should have all of your stuff out of the office by close of business today.'[194]

Ambassador Jones corroborated Maxwell's version of events. She testified that Deputy Assistant Secretary Elizabeth Dibble informed her of Secretary Clinton's decision regarding Maxwell. Jones testified:

> Q. [Y]ou learned from Liz Dibble, who learned from Cheryl Mills, that the Secretary had determined that [Maxwell] should be relieved of his duties. Is that correct?
>
> A. That he should be removed as DAS.
>
> Q. Removed as DAS.
>
> A. That is correct.[195]

Jones was clear that the decision to remove Maxwell came from Secretary Clinton herself, not the ARB. She testified:

---

[193] Gordon & Schmitt, *supra* note 28.
[194] Maxwell Tr. at 29.
[195] Jones Tr. at 90.

Q.   And to be clear, to your understanding, it wasn't the ARB that was recommending that these individuals be placed on administrative leave, this is something that came from the Department itself? Is that your understanding?

A.   That was my understanding. At that point I had not read the classified ARB. I had read the unclassified. And of course, this was not present in -- the issue of the personnel issue was not in the unclassified. So I -- the only reason that I knew of by -- as explained to Liz -- was that the Secretary herself had been upset to hear -- to read that Ray Maxwell had not been reading intelligence for quite a while and that this was not acceptable.[196]

Jones disagreed with the Department's decision to remove Maxwell from his position, but did not contest the decision. She testified:

Q.   What was your reaction when you learned that he had been named for those reasons in the ARB?

A.   What I knew, what I was told, because at the time I was asked to have the conversation with Ray, I had not read the classified. So I did not know what it said. I was told what it said. I did not believe that that warranted his removal as DAS, no.

Q.   Did you question anybody about that?

A.   No.

Q.   At any point?

A.   No.[197]

Another individual named by the ARB, Assistant Secretary for DS Eric Boswell, told the Committee that Under Secretary for Management Patrick Kennedy informed him that the ARB had included him in the report. Boswell immediately submitted a letter of resignation. He stated:

I received a phone call from Under Secretary Kennedy, and I don't remember the exact date, but that's the date the report came out. He said, the report is awful, and it has criticized you, Scott Bultrowicz, Ray Maxwell, who was a Deputy Assistant Secretary in the NEA Bureau, and Charlene Lamb, and has recommended that you be removed from your position. When I heard that news, I was shocked. I went back to my office to think things over. I was in my office actually. I hung up the phone to

---

[196] *Id.* at 77.
[197] *Id.* at 89.

think things over. And I called Kennedy back up, asked for an appointment, got it. I walked up there to his office and with my letter of resignation, which had I written out by hand. And so I resigned.[198]

* * *

When I learned of this finding, I decided I had little choice, I think. I decided to resign because I wanted to resign on my terms. I didn't feel that the verdict, if you like, was justified; that I wasn't going to [sic] wait to be pushed. And so that's why I resigned. My resignation was not asked for, but I won't speculate as to what was going to happen next. I was, I should say, asked to stay on as Director of the Office of Foreign Missions.[199]

Kennedy accepted Boswell's resignation, but convinced him to remain with the Department as the Director of the Office of Foreign Missions, a title that Boswell held in addition to his role as Assistant Secretary for DS. Within days, Boswell and the others were placed on administrative leave.

The State Department took unreasonable actions with respect to placing four officials on administrative leave.

The four individuals relieved of their duties were told that their leave status would be temporary. It would last only until the Department was able to find another position to move them into. Ultimately, however, the four were relegated to bureaucratic purgatory where they remained, at taxpayer expense, for eight months while the Department decided their futures.

When Ambassador Jones informed Maxwell of the Secretary's decision that he was to be relieved of his duties, he was told that it was a temporary situation. Maxwell testified:

> [Jones] said, 'Don't worry, this is going to be temporary.' She told me, 'We will bring you back as a Senior Adviser. We will have an office space for you.' In fact, she said, 'I will have Liz arrange an office space for you today so that you could move your things to so you don't have to take them home.'[200]

Jones similarly recalled the conversation. She stated:

> I asked Ray [Maxwell] to come see me that day after getting that instruction and explained to him what I had been told, that it was because he had not been reading intelligence that this - the decision

---

[198] Boswell Tr. at 33.
[199] *Id.* at 34.
[200] Maxwell Tr. at 28.

had been made, that I was very surprised that he hadn't been reading intelligence. And he -- but that, **from what I understood, that the arrangement was that he would be removed from his DAS responsibilities but that he would remain in NEA**. I told him that, as far as I was concerned, he was a good and valuable colleague, that we would definitely find useful, honorable work for him to do in NEA, that there were many, many issues that were important to us, that -- he expressed at that point a particular interest in working on the North Africa Sahel issues, and I said, well, that might be a possibility and that I would certainly pursue that and that we would definitely have a nice office for him and that he should please stay with us.[201]

Elizabeth Dibble was also led to believe that Maxwell would be removed from his position but that he would remain with NEA. She stated:

Q. At the time that this all happened, what was your understanding of what would happen to Mr. Maxwell?

A. **That he would be reassigned to a non-DAS position in NEA. That he would stay in the Bureau.**[202]

Ambassador Boswell described a similar experience. Shortly after Kennedy asked Boswell to retain his concurrent position as the Director of the Office of Foreign Missions, he was placed on administrative leave anyways. Boswell testified:

Q. After you had your meeting with Under Secretary Kennedy, he asked you to stay on in your other capacity. About how long after that did you hear from him again?

A. Days, but I don't remember exactly how long.

Q. And he just -- days later you received a call from him saying you've been placed on administrative leave?

A. I received a call from him that said, you're going to be notified that you are being placed on administrative leave, as are the three other people.

Q. And who made that decision?

A. I don't know.

Q. **Did he provide any context or any additional information?**

---

[201] Jones Tr. at 74.
[202] Dibble Tr. at 81 (emphasis added).

A.   **Beyond saying he didn't think it would last long.**[203]

* * *

Q.   So you were asked to stay on and then placed on administrative leave?

A.   That's right, days between that time.

Q.   That one's a little hard for me to wrap my head around. Can you provide some context to that?

A.   I don't have any other context. **I was totally astonished.**

Q.   Who informed you of that?

A.   Under Secretary Kennedy.

Q.   Who asked you to stay on?

A.   Under Secretary Kennedy. Who informed me of that I would be put on administrative leave?

Q.   Yes.

A.   Under Secretary Kennedy.

Q.   Who asked to you stay on prior to being put on [administrative leave]?

A.   Under Secretary Kennedy.

Q.   Did he give you any explanation for why you were being put on administrative leave?

A.   No.[204]

Senior State Department officials informed Ambassador Boswell and the others affected that they had been placed on administrative leave and that they should expect this to be a temporary situation while the Department conducted its own performance evaluations.

---

[203] Boswell Tr. at 95-96.
[204] Boswell Tr. at 34-35.

***The administrative leave process was haphazard and unfamiliar to the
employees directly affected by it.***

When Ambassador Jones learned that Maxwell was being placed on administrative leave—specifically that he had been told to give up his badge and computer—she complained to Ambassador Kennedy and others that the actions taken by the Department did not comport with what she had been told would happen to Maxwell. She testified:

> Then on a Saturday morning, I had a -- I can't now remember if it was an e-mail or a call from Ray saying that he was extremely upset, that he had gotten a letter that he had been asked to sign saying he was on administrative leave and that this meant that he had to give up his badge and his BlackBerry access, his computer access. And I said, no, **that's not at all what I was told, that none of that was meant to happen, that that was quite the contrary to what I'd been told, and that I would get it fixed**.
>
> **So I called several people, Director General Pat Kennedy, people like that, and said, this is not at all what the understanding was, this is not at all what I was told when you asked me to remove Ray as DAS but he would stay in NEA. This is not at all what you told me was the case when you said that this was going to be changed to administrative leave. I strenuously object to this.** This is not at all what was agreed and this is not appropriate, from my perspective, in this situation. And we got it changed so he did not lose his badge and he did not lose his computer access.[205]

Ambassador Jones told the Committee she did not believe that Maxwell should have been placed on administrative leave. She testified:

> Q. Okay. As his supervisor, do you believe that Mr. Maxwell's conduct merited his being relieved of duties as DAS?
>
> A. No.
>
> Q. Do you believe, as his supervisor, that his conduct merited his being placed on administrative leave?
>
> A. No.[206]

Dibble also agreed with Jones that a failure to participate in the daily intelligence reading would not warrant administrative leave. She testified:

---

[205] Jones Tr. at 75-77.
[206] Jones Tr. at 89.

Q. I know you also talked at the end a little bit about if you had been aware that Mr. Maxwell wasn't reading this material that you would have recommended that his supervisor, Beth Jones, speak to him about it. Do you think not reading it would warrant administrative leave?

A. No. Absolutely not.[207]

The Secretary's decision to place the four employees on administrative leave created substantial uncertainty for the employees and their relevant supervisors. In fact, senior Department officials and supervisors interviewed by the Committee could not even describe the administrative leave process. When asked to describe her understanding of the process, Ambassador Jones testified:

Q. Can we go just back to the administrative leave issue? As a supervisor in the State Department with a lot of experience, what is your understanding of the purpose of administrative leave?

A. When I was first told that a decision had been made to move the four into administrative leave, I asked, because **I didn't know what administrative leave means, and I was told in this situation all it meant was that they would not be coming to work, but that they would be getting full pay, that they would not -- and that the arrangements that I had discussed with Ray Maxwell to move him into a different position in NEA were no longer operative**.

Q. And who told you this? Do you recall?

A. I don't recall specifically, no.

Q. Okay. Have you ever had to put anyone on administrative leave before? Not in this situation, but in other situations in your experience?

A. I don't believe I have ever, no.

* * *

Q. Is it your opinion it's a fairly routine measure or is it fairly uncommon? Just your opinion.

A. **In my experience it's uncommon.** [208]

---

[207] Dibble Tr. at 68-69.
[208] Jones Tr. at 156-57.

Jones' deputy, Principal Deputy Assistant Secretary Elizabeth Dibble was also unfamiliar with the administrative leave process. Dibble testified:

> Q. You're a supervisor essentially at the State Department, is that fair to say?
>
> A. Yes.
>
> Q. **I'm just trying to determine what the purpose of administrative leave is in the State Department, typically?**
>
> A. **That's a tough question. I don't know.** I mean, it's -- I have never placed anyone on administrative leave, and I've never had anyone who was working for me on administrative leave. It is, you know, sometimes used, I believe, if someone, for instance, loses a security clearance or something like that. But I don't know.
>
> Q. Have you ever heard of anybody being placed on administrative leave for as long as Mr. Maxwell has been placed on administrative leave?
>
> A. No, I don't know -- I don't really know much about administrative leave. So, no.[209]

State Department employees and their supervisors were left in the dark about any personnel reviews being undertaken on the four employees placed on administrative leave, or why the reviews have taken so long. Boswell repeatedly tried to obtain an update from the Department on his status:

> Q. Okay. It is now, what, 6 months later?
>
> A. Yes.
>
> Q. And you said you've inquired every couple of weeks as to what your status is?
>
> A. Correct. I wouldn't say every couple of weeks, but from time to time.
>
> Q. Okay. And no response?
>
> A. No response -- well, beyond saying it is still under advisement.
>
> Q. So what is your understanding of the process right now; what is happening?

---

[209] Dibble Tr. at 85-86.

A.   My understanding of the process is that at some point the Secretary
        of State is going to have to decide whether myself and the three
        others remain on administrative leave or not.

Q.   Why is it taking this long?

A.   I can't answer that. "I don't know" is the answer.

Q.   Have you ever seen something like this –

A.   No.

Q.   -- in your experience at the State Department?

A.   No, I have not.[210]

As of July 9, 2013, the date of Bultrowicz's interview with the Committee, the
Department had effectively provided him with no information about his administrative leave
status, when he might return to work, and what, if any, additional investigation the Department
was undertaking. Bultrowicz described his experience to the Committee. He stated:

Q.   When were you placed on administrative leave?

A.   December 21st.

Q.   So it's been, what, 6 months?

A.   Yeah, a little over -- it will be 7 months in July, July 21st.

Q.   What have you been told as far as how long that status will last?

A.   Until a decision is made.

Q.   Do you know –

A.   So, I mean, I don't know. I was not given a specific length of time.

Q.   Do you know how the decision is going to be made as far as what to do?

A.   No.

Q.   Do you know who is the decider?

A.   Again, I mean, it's just -- I would imagine maybe the Secretary. I'm not sure.

---

[210] Boswell Tr. at 95-96.

Q. Do you know if the State Department is doing any sort of additional investigation or internal review to make the decision?

A. No.

Q. Do you know if they're relying on anything besides what's in the unclassified ARB report?

A. No.

Q. Have they given you any sort of –

A. I mean, I would imagine that, in making their decision, other than the classified ARB report, they would look at your performance record, assignments, I mean, that type of thing. So I'm sure there is supporting documentation they're looking at, not looking at solely the declassified ARB. I would think. I am not sure.

Q. Do you have any idea if they are doing additional interviews or kind of crosschecking any of the findings in the ARB report?

A. I'm not aware of that, no.[211]

Jones, as Maxwell's supervisor, has also not been privy to information or updates about Maxwell's status. She testified:

Q. And what's your understanding as to what the process is now insofar as Mr. Maxwell is concerned? Is this something that you're privy to?

A. I have no understanding of it at all. I just know that -- what I've been told, which is that he still remains on administrative leave, that they all remain on administrative leave. But it's not a process that I'm privy to.[212]

The fact that a supervisor has no visibility into the Department's evaluation of an employee under her supervision begs the question of how the Department evaluated the performance of these individuals. Secretary Kerry's performance review does not appear to have included interviews with the supervisors of the officials placed on administrative leave.

Ambassador Jones told the Committee that she disagreed with the decision to place all four individuals on administrative leave. She also could not explain why the process has taken so long. She stated:

---

[211] Bultrowicz Tr. at 149-150
[212] Jones Tr. at 77.

Q.   Do you have any concerns with respect to Mr. Maxwell, how he's been treated with respect to his administrative leave?

A.   I don't think any of them should have been put on administrative leave, including Ray.

Q.   Do you have any idea why Mr. Maxwell is still on administrative leave?

A.   I don't know.

Q.   And have you ever heard of anyone being placed on administrative leave for as long as Mr. Maxwell has been on administrative leave?

A.   I have so little experience with administrative leave I really can't say.[213]

Though the four employees were told the period of administrative leave would be far shorter—only long enough to find a new placement. Instead, they remained in administrative limbo for approximately eight months. While on administrative leave neither the four employees nor their supervisors received updates as to the status of the personnel investigations. More troublingly, as discussed below, the State Department severely restricted access to the classified ARB report and the employees were given no chance to appeal or otherwise discuss the findings of the ARB, findings which resulted in their being placed on administrative leave.

The State Department severely restricted access to the classified version of the ARB report.

The State Department has restricted access to the classified ARB report by limiting its availability to career officials who were placed on administrative leave. The classified report, which contains additional detailed findings of the actions of Boswell, Bultrowicz, Lamb, and Maxwell, also recommends administrative action for two of those four individuals. Despite this, however, for six months many of the employees on administrative leave were forbidden access to the classified report. The first time some of them were able to view the report was in preparation for their interviews with Committee staff. Ray Maxwell testified about when he first read the classified report. He stated:

I also find it strange, if not mystifying, that **the State Department would intentionally prohibit me access for six months to the details of the now-declassified allegation**, the charges against me for which I had been already been unjustly punished, **until just yesterday, when my attorney**

---

[213] Jones Tr. at 157-158.

and I were first allowed to view pertinent portions of the classified ARB Report.[214]

Scott Bultrowicz repeatedly asked for access to the classified report so he could better understand exactly why he was put on administrative leave. The State Department repeatedly denied his request. The first time Bultrowicz viewed the classified report was shortly before his interview with Committee staff. He testified:

> Q. Did you ever try to reach out to anybody whether it's members of the ARB or Under Secretary Kennedy, or others in what would be your chain of command, and sit down and say hey, you know, help me understand what I have done wrong here, help me understand how I can avoid this in the future, what is my status of coming back? That is a lot of questions.

> A. Well, when I would get calls from the department, it typically was to give me updates on my status, which, again, was still in review. As far as asking, you know, what I did wrong, I mean, that was a question. Saying, you know, **every time I spoke to someone, I said, look, I haven't been able to see the ARB or its findings specifically in regards to me. I would like to see it.** And it was eventually produced last week

> Q. And what reason were you given for why you couldn't see the ARB, either the classified version or just the portion on the finding? I assume, given your role, you had clearance level available to read the classified ARB?

> A. **I was told that it was actually being, you know, very tightly controlled**, and I think even you have to say though, and this is something that I think the department was probably trying to do its best to protect employees, is there's the classified ARB, which I read, and there's not much difference, not a lot of difference between the unclassified and classified. There is a bit more substance, I think, but I think key to it was protecting the privacy of the personnel who the ARB cited in its findings. So I know there wasn't at least a wide distribution of that.[215]

Political appointees and more senior officials within the State Department, however, had seemingly unfettered access to the classified report. Assistant Secretary Eric Boswell, who, like Bultrowicz and Maxwell was placed on administrative leave as a result of the report's findings, was able to review the classified report as soon as it came out. Boswell stated:

---

[214] Maxwell Tr. at 152.
[215] Bultrowicz Tr. at 80-81.

Q. Did you have an opportunity to read the report or passages about you?

A. **I asked for the opportunity to read the report.** I had already resigned, I had submitted my letter of resignation. I said I thought it was only fair to read what they said about me, because I didn't know, **so he said, of course.** I obtained a copy of the report, the full report. I was moving very fast; I did not read the full report. I went to the accountability section, and I read that thoroughly, and then I thumbed through the rest of the report.

Q.   That was the day –

A. **The day of, day of. I think that was the day that the report was made available to the Department, but it may have been the following day.**

Q.   So you did have an opportunity to review the classified version?

A. I did.   Again, it was a very quick review.   I was concentrating on what they had to say about me.[216]

Likewise, Acting Assistant Secretary Beth Jones, who was not disciplined, was able to review the classified report whenever she wanted. She testified:

Q. When did you first have an opportunity to read the classified ARB?

A.   I didn't. I read it this week.

Q. Okay. Was it provided in advance of preparation for this interview?

A.   Yes. **Well, I asked for it. I had plenty of opportunities to read it**, and each time I had scheduled to read it, it was overtaken by a crisis that I had to deal with right now. I didn't have the luxury of sitting down and reading it.

Q.   So you had requested to read it prior to this past week?

A.   Absolutely. **And I had scheduled to read it many times.**[217]

Ambassador Jones was out of the office the morning the ARB report was delivered to the Secretary. As a result, Cheryl Mills called Principal Deputy Secretary of State for Near Eastern

---

[216] Boswell Tr. at 86-87.
[217] Jones Tr. at 96-97.

Affairs, Elizabeth Dibble, into her office to read the report and learn of the findings. Dibble testified:

> Q. Moving forward with your experience with the ARB, after the report came out, when did you first learn that individuals had been cited for criticism?

> A. I learned the morning that the report was going to be released that there were individuals, including one of my colleagues, who was going to be.

> Q. And how did you learn this?

> A. **I received a call from Cheryl Mills, who asked me to come up to her office and gave me a copy of the classified version of the report,** because, of course, the personnel stuff doesn't appear in the unclassified version, and she had me stay and read it there. And as I recall, Beth Jones was -- she was traveling, she was not in the office that morning for some reason. **Otherwise Beth would have gotten the call from Cheryl. But this is one of these cases where the PDAS takes over for the assistant secretary.**

> Q. And what was the purpose of having you read it at that point?

> A. So that I knew -- so that NEA new. **And she told me I could -- I should brief Beth, but I was not to discuss this further**, that NEA knew what was in the report and how our Bureau and DS were being characterized.[218]

Dibble was personally asked by the Chief of Staff to review the classified report in the absence of Ambassador Jones. Yet when Scott Bultrowicz, who served in the State Department at the same level as Dibble, asked to review the classified report to understand the basis of his removal and placement on administrative leave, he was denied access to it.

The employees placed on administrative leave were denied due process.

The lack of access to the classified ARB report—especially by those placed on administrative leave as a result of the report—and the administrative leave process itself denied Boswell, Bultrowicz, Lamb, and Maxwell of their due process rights. This is in stark contrast to the State Department's public acknowledgement of the importance of the due process rights of the employees on leave. On May 20, 2013, State Department spokesman Patrick Ventrell said:

---

[218] Dibble Tr. at 77-78.

It's important to remember we're dealing with four individuals who -- that we discussed are long-serving government officials who over the years have provided dedicated service to the U.S. government in challenging assignments. And career Foreign Service employees are entitled to due process and legal protection under the Foreign Service Act, with respect to any potential disciplinary actions.[219]

The ARB did not question the officials held accountable in the ARB report about the conduct for which they were criticized.

Multiple employees who were relieved of their duties and placed on administrative leave as a result of the findings by the ARB testified that the ARB never asked them about the issues for which the panel later criticized them. Similarly, supervisors were not questioned by the ARB about the actions of their subordinates.

Eric Boswell, who was cited for his failures as a supervisor, testified that the ARB never asked him about his actions as a supervisor. He stated:

A.   Yeah, I was the -- it's not the first time I've been before an ARB. In the first meeting my recollection was simply a general discussion of this sort of set-up, just as we have had here at the outset of this meeting. At the final or the last meeting that we had, it was relatively brief, it was cordial, it was quite friendly. **I don't remember exactly the line of questioning, but I do remember that there was no questioning about my role as a supervisor, none at all.** There was no indication of what conclusions the ARB was coming to, not a clue of any of these, any conclusions. **And there was -- as I say, I was talking about what was not asked -- there was no conversation about my supervision . . .**

Q.   **So no questions about the actions of your subordinates, or your role in supervising them, or anything –**

A.   **Not that I recall, no.[220]**

Not only did Boswell testify that he was never asked about his role as a supervisor, but he testified that the ARB never asked him about the actions of the individuals under his supervision that were ultimately criticized by the ARB. He stated:

Q.   Did they ask you questions about Ms. Lamb?

A.   I don't recall if they asked me questions about Ms. Lamb, Ms. Lamb's

[219] Statement of Patrick Ventrell, Acting Deputy Spokesperson, U.S. Dep't of State, Press Briefing (May 20, 2013).
[220] Boswell Tr. at 32-33 (emphasis added).

management style.

> Q. But did they ask you questions in general about Ms. Lamb?
>
> A. I don't recall that they did.[221]

Scott Bultrowicz testified that the ARB never asked him about the topics for which the panel later criticized him. Bultrowicz testified:

> Q. And that was going to be my followup, was you know, they asked you about your relationship with Assistant Secretary Boswell and a few others, but **did they ask you any questions that really drove at the things that you are being criticized for?**
>
> A. **No.**
>
> Q. Okay. No one has been able to give you any clarity as to why that decision was made?
>
> A. No.
>
> Q. I just imagine that is very frustrating for you.
>
> A. **It's frustrating.**[222]
>
> * * *
>
> Q Why do you think the ARB got that wrong then? Why did they get it wrong if you believe that their characterization of you is wrong? How did they come across that wrong characterization?
>
> A I don't know. I mean, I don't have access to, you know, maybe 10 people came in and said, boy, that Scott Bultrowicz, he just really doesn't know what he is doing. I don't know.
>
> Q Only taking into consideration your testimony to the ARB, what could they have done in order to clarify that in your eyes in front of you?
>
> A They could have asked me. You know, what steps.
>
> Q And what are the questions they didn't ask?
>
> A All right, if it was an issue with a particular employee, what steps did you take? Well, I can tell you when I came in with all of my

---

[221] *Id.* at 73.
[222] Bultrowicz Tr. at 82.

assistant directors, or DAS's, I instituted one-on-one meetings with them every week. Sometimes if we couldn't make it, it would skip a week, but the door was always open. There was always discussion. I saw my DAS's, my directorates. We had threat meetings, or threat briefings every morning. We had small staff meetings every week. We had large staff meetings. I mean, engagement was not an issue. All right, so that's one thing. And again, I would go back and say, what is the expectation of the department in overseeing a Deputy Assistant Secretary? Okay.

Secondly, as far as being proactive, well, they could have asked me[,] since you became director, what have you done? And I could have listed off that, you know, we redirected resources from Iraq to Libya, positions, not only agents, but also security protective specialists, which what made it so difficult, is those positions were funded through supplemental funding, specifically for Iraq. So we had to go through a lot of red tape so that those were readjusted, reassigned, reprogrammed, which we eventually did. The FACT training, the high-threat training. There are a lot of things that we were doing proactively to help the situation in Libya. And that could have been asked.[223]

Bultrowicz testified that the ARB had an opportunity to question him about his supervision, yet did not. He stated:

No, look. Here is my thing. I will take responsibility for the decisions I made based on the information I had at hand, okay. I mean, and I'm not looking to point the finger, you know. Accountability cuts a wide swath, I think. So I'm not saying I had nothing to do with this. I mean, it would be shame on me if I said I was completely oblivious to everything. I'm willing to take responsibility for the decisions I made based on the information I had. But, you know, to say, well, you should have managed person A more closely, or you should have been more proactive, that's pretty general to me. And I mean, you know, it is what it is. I respect the members of that panel. They are all very distinguished officials. **But yeah, I have a problem with it. I do. I don't think it's something that defines me after 27 years of doing everything I'm asked, or at least to say be more direct in the questioning with me when they had the opportunity.**[224]

Ray Maxwell also testified that the ARB never asked him about their concerns about his actions with respect to the daily intelligence book. He stated:

[223] *Id.* at 96-98.
[224] Bultrowicz Tr. at 81-82.

I continue to find it most puzzling that ARB would attach so much significance to the now-declassified allegation that resulted in my removal and six months of administrative leave without double-checking with me to make sure it was true or valid or relevant or even properly characterized. **If I had been in their shoes, I would certainly have checked if I were going to attach so much significance to it.**[225]

The evidence and testimony provided to the Committee to date suggests that the ARB's findings and recommendations regarding accountability were made without the benefit of testimony from the accused employees, or their supervisors, on the very topics for which they were criticized. These witnesses were not questioned on the topics that became the basis for their administrative leave, and entered their administrative leave confused, angry, and frustrated.

The employees placed on administrative leave were not given an opportunity to respond to the allegations against them.

Not only did these witnesses not have a chance to engage the ARB directly on the issues for which the ARB criticized them, but they were also unable to undertake any formal process to challenge the criticisms—or even review them at all. The State Department kept these employees completely in the dark regarding their administrative leave status. The Department, in contrast to two hundred years of settled jurisprudence and constitutional writing, also denied them the opportunity to face their accusers and respond to their allegations.

By placing the four employees on indefinite administrative leave, the State Department prevented the accused employees from formally challenging the ARB's findings and recommendations. According to Boswell, the State Department has given him no opportunity to appeal the decision to place him on administrative leave, or to challenge the ARB's findings and recommendations. Boswell stated:

Q. And you have been given no opportunity to, if you will, face your accusers or respond to the allegations against you?

A. I have not.

Q. Is there any avenue from which you can do that?

A. I'm not aware of any.

Q. There's no appeal process that you can go through or –

A. To answer your question, **there's no appeal process that I know of. I'm a bit disappointed that I didn't have a chance during the ARB, if they were coming to a conclusion, the conclusion that they did, to ask me about it and ask my views about that**

---

[225] Maxwell Tr. at 152 (emphasis added).

judgment. That would happen if you were being -- in any other kind of review done by inspectors or GAO or whatever, you get an opportunity to comment. I didn't get an opportunity to comment; I just saw the conclusion, surprised to see the conclusion.[226]

Scott Bultrowicz testified that he is unsure of what information the State Department used, in addition to the ARB report, to evaluate his status as an employee. Bultrowicz stated:

> Q. Do you know if the State Department is doing any sort of additional investigation or internal review to make the decision?
>
> A. No.
>
> Q. **Do you know if they're relying on anything besides what's in the unclassified ARB report?**
>
> A. **No.** I mean, I would imagine that, in making their decision, other than the classified ARB report, they would look at your performance record, assignments, I mean, that type of thing. **So I'm sure there is supporting documentation they're looking at, not looking at solely the declassified ARB. I would think. I am not sure.**
>
> Q. Do you have any idea if they are doing additional interviews or kind of crosschecking any of the findings in the ARB report?
>
> A. I'm not aware of that, no.
>
> Q. Is there any indication that your testimony today has any bearing on the decision to remove you from admin leave?
>
> A. No.[227]

Ray Maxwell testified that he was not even aware of what the charges were against him for months after he was first placed on administrative leave. Maxwell stated:

> Well, I guess we should start that discussion with the fact that we only got access to the classified version of the report yesterday. This is after asking for the past six months for it. **So, for six months, I was in the administrative-leave status, which amounts to sort of a punitive measure without knowing what the charge was.**[228]

---

[226] Boswell Tr. at 98

[227] Bultrowicz Tr. at 150-151.

[228] Maxwell Tr. at 42.

88

Maxwell testified that the process was unfair, and that he was not given any due process regarding his administrative leave status. This, according to Maxwell, was against State Department rules. He stated:

> **I was removed from the DAS position in violation of a number of rules that exist for removing a person involuntarily from a position in Washington**, and the rules--the Foreign Affairs Manual Rules are very clear about how you go about removing a person from a position. There is a procedure that's established, and that procedure exists for a reason: To provide a sort of fairness and due process.
>
> **There was no fairness. There was no due process in the way I was removed from my position.**[229]

All of the employees placed on administrative leave by the Department who were questioned by Committee staff found the administrative leave process confusing and unfair. That sentiment was shared by colleagues throughout the State Department. Maxwell stated that a human resources official felt he had been sufficiently punished and lamented that she was unable to provide him with answers when he asked for status updates. Maxwell testified:

A. No. I have no visibility on the process. I don't know who is involved with the process. I don't know at what stage we are at in the process. I know nothing about it.

Q. Do you have a person that you contact regularly or periodically to--

A. I check in with the Director General.

* * *

Q. And what does she tell you?

A. She tells me, "Ray, we're still working on it. "Ray," she always says--her position is that the administrative leave period should end and we should all be brought back to work.

Q. I'm sorry? That's her--

A. Her position is that the administrative leave period should end and we should all be brought back to work. In fact, she say she has-- she's told me and she's told Pat Kennedy--in fact, she told Cheryl Mills before she left, "We punished these people enough.

---

[229] *Id.* at 129.

They need to be brought back to work." But she hasn't prevailed because the administrative leave has continued.[230]

According to the testimony of the four officials placed on leave, none were told how long their administrative leave would last. According to their testimony, none were able to formally rebut the allegations against them. According to their testimony, none were even questioned by the ARB about the reasons they were ultimately placed on administrative leave.

Despite public proclamations by the State Department that these employees were entitled to due process under the Foreign Service Act, these employees *did not* in fact receive due process.

The State Department is Back to Business as Usual

Nine months after the ARB report was released and four employees were relieved of their duties and subsequently placed on administrative leave, little has changed at the State Department. In August 2013, Secretary Kerry determined that all four employees would be reinstated.

The decision to place the four officials on administrative leave was touted as a step towards holding accountable those individuals who bore responsibility for the inadequate security posture in Benghazi. The facts, however, paint a much different picture. The Department simply reacted to the findings of the ARB and, in the process, created the illusion of accountability. Assistant Secretary Beth Jones testified that she didn't know why the four officials were placed on administrative leave, but had heard that it was necessary to "regularize their status." She stated:

> Q. Do you know how he was placed on administrative leave then? Were you part of that?
>
> A. I was not part of the decision on that. I was told the following. I don't remember the timeframe exactly but it was still before Christmas. [...] I heard from the director general's office that a decision was being made to move the four to administrative leave, and I talked to the deputy director general about what that meant. **And he said it doesn't mean anything different from what we had told them originally, that nothing at all would change. It was just a way to regularize their status.**[231]

"Regularizing their status" afforded the Department an opportunity to show the public that it was actively taking steps to hold people accountable for the Benghazi attacks. In reality,

---

[230] Maxwell Tr. at 139.

[231] Jones Tr. at 75-76.

however, the Department was just biding its time before it went back to business as usual. Last month, after eight months of these four employees receiving full pay on administrative leave, Secretary Kerry reinstated them and determined that they would not face any formal disciplinary action. As Chairman Issa said at the time Secretary Kerry made this announcement:

> It is now clear that the personnel actions taken by the Department in response to the Benghazi terrorist attacks was more of a public relations strategy than a measured response to a failure in leadership.[232]

In fact, two of these employees had previously announced their retirement, but chose not to retire under the stigma of administrative leave. Ambassador Boswell testified:

> I had always planned to retire at the end of the last administration. I had been Assistant Secretary for many years. It's a meat grinder of a job, and I had always planned to retire. That was well known. I had told Under Secretary Kennedy and others that at the end of the Clinton administration, having served two -- actually three administrations, I planned to retire.

> Actually 'retire' is the wrong word, the word is 'resign,' because I am already a retired Foreign Service officer -- but to resign my commissions as Assistant Secretary and Director of the Office of Foreign Missions, but once I was put on administrative leave, I made the personal decision that I did not want to resign a commission under these circumstances, that I wanted my situation resolved before I took another step.

> When you asked me what the effect on my life, it has been a profound effect, a profoundly deleterious effect on my life. [...] I had planned -- had various plans to move on. All of those are on the shelf. And so it is perhaps the most painful period of my professional life.[233]

Maxwell told the Committee that if he had just been fired he would have had an opportunity to contest the decision. Instead, he and the other affected employees have been left in limbo. As a result, he delayed plans for retirement in order to contest the Department's actions. He stated:

> Q. Do you believe that you have been subject to an adverse action within the Department of State?

> A. Yes, definitely.

> Q. What would you say to those in the Department of State and the officials who would claim that you were not technically subject to an adverse action?

> A. There are people who will say that because they'll say you're still

---

[232] Press release, Hon. Darrell Issa, Chairman, H. Comm. on Oversight and Gov't Reform (Aug. 20, 2013).
[233] Boswell Tr. at 97-98.

getting paid, and because you're still getting paid, you don't have any reason to complain. But you know, it's not about the money. It's about your reason for being, if you will. And, you know, frankly, I would have been better off had they said you are fired from the State Department. You go today. Your pay stops, and you're out of here. I would have been better off because I could have contested that or--I mean, I would have contested it. It would have also been behind. It would have all been behind me and I could have started with the next thing. But as things now stand, I'm still employed. There's still a possibility that I could come back, so it's not like I can start something new.

I was scheduled to retire on April 30th, and I made the decision to withdraw my retirement request because I didn't want to go out under this cloud of suspicion that maybe I had done something, that's the cloud that--my fear of the cloud of suspicion no longer exists because I have embraced my administrative leave-ness, if you will, and it's no longer a source of shame for me. It's now-- almost--it's increasingly becoming a source of pride for me. So, it's not that big a deal anymore. But now there's a principle. Now there's a principle that they did something improperly, immorally, maybe even illegally, and if I just take it laying down, guess what, they'll do it to somebody else again.[234]

According to information obtained by the Committee, two other employees—Charlene Lamb and Scott Bultrowicz—are currently being considered for prestigious assignments overseas.

Conclusion

The unclassified ARB report begins with a quote from George Santayana's 1905 book, *Reason in Common Sense*: "Those that cannot remember the past are condemned to repeat it." Notwithstanding this promising start, the gaps in the ARB review and final report identified by the Committee signal that the State Department may very well be doomed to repeat its past mistakes.

In response to a question about Benghazi at a May 13, 2013 press conference, the President pledged to the American people to "find out what happened."[235] To this day, more than one year after the attacks, not a single person at the State Department has actually been fired or formally held accountable for the attacks in Benghazi. More importantly, those most accountable for the attacks in Benghazi—the terrorists who attacked U.S. facilities and claimed the lives of four Americans—have not been brought to justice.

---

[234] Maxwell Tr. at 121-122.

[235] Remarks of President Barack Obama at a joint press conference with Prime Minister David Cameron (May 13, 2013).

The gaps in the ARB's work are particularly troubling because the Obama Administration has repeatedly touted the ARB report as the final word on failures by the State Department that contributed to the inadequate security posture in Benghazi. The limitations inherent in the ARB's mandate and the weaknesses in the ARB's methodology show that a more thorough investigation is necessary. The Committee will continue to examine the events before, during and after the September 11, 2012 attacks on U.S. diplomatic facilities to properly assign accountability and to make findings that will inform legislative remedies.

Appendix

On May 20, 2013 the State Department released an update on the efforts to implement the ARB's recommendations. The ARB issued 29 recommendations (24 of which were unclassified) to the Department of State. A brief summary of the Department's actions on the 24 unclassified recommendations is as follows:[236]

1. The Department must strengthen security for personnel and platforms beyond traditional reliance on host government security support in high risk, high threat posts.

   - *The Department established a High Threat Board to review our presence at High Threat, High Risk posts; the Board will review these posts every 6 months.*
   - *We created a Deputy Assistant Secretary for High Threat Posts in the Bureau of Diplomatic Security (DS), who is responsible for ensuring that such posts receive the focused attention they need.*

2. The Board recommends that the Department re-examine DS organization and management, with a particular emphasis on span of control for security policy planning for all overseas U.S. diplomatic facilities.

   - *The Department established a six-person panel to thoroughly review DS's organization and management structure; the panel has developed draft findings.*

3. Regional bureaus should have augmented support within the bureau on security matters, to include a senior DS officer to report to the regional Assistant Secretary.

   - *DS staff attend regular Regional Bureau meetings, and Regional Bureau staff attend DS daily briefings to better communicate on security issues.*
   - *The Department has adjusted the work requirements (position descriptions) for senior level staff (Assistant Secretaries and Deputy Assistant Secretaries) to reflect everyone's responsibility for overseas security.*

4. The Department should establish a panel of outside independent experts (military, security, humanitarian) with experience in high risk, high threat areas to identify best practices (from other agencies and other countries), and evaluate U.S. security platforms in high risk, high threat posts.

   - *The Department established a six-person panel to identify best practices used by other agencies and countries; this panel's work is expected to be complete by late summer.*

5. The Department should develop minimum security standards for occupancy of temporary facilities in high risk, high threat environments, and seek greater flexibility to make funds rapidly available for security upgrades at such facilities.

---

[236] Fact Sheet, "Benghazi Accountability Review Board Implementation," State Department Office of the Spokesperson (May 20, 2013).

- *The Department has re-affirmed that Overseas Security Policy Board Standards apply to temporary facilities.*
- *We identified flexible funding authorities to make improvements to our overseas facilities.*

6. Before opening or re-opening critical threat or high risk, high threat posts, the Department should establish a multi-bureau support cell, residing in the regional bureau.

- *The Department developed standard operating procedures for "Support Cells" for opened/reopened posts. The process is being incorporated into the Foreign Affairs Handbook.*

7. All State Department and other government agencies' facilities should be collocated when they are in the same metropolitan area, unless a waiver has been approved.

- *We verified all data on our overseas facilities; we are exploring which non-collocated facilities can be eliminated and their personnel relocated.*

8. The Secretary should require an action plan from DS, OBO, and other relevant offices on the use of fire as a weapon against diplomatic facilities, including immediate steps to deal with urgent issues.

- *The Department issued guidance to all posts on "weapons of opportunity."*
- *Fire testing is ongoing at U.S. military facilities.*

9. The Department should revise its guidance to posts and require key offices to perform in-depth status checks of post tripwires.

- *The Department reviewed and revised requirements for posts on how to respond to changing security benchmarks (i.e., "tripwires").*
- *The Department established a Washington-based "Tripwires Committee" to review tripwires upon breach, to help ensure that posts and regional bureaus in Washington respond more quickly should security deteriorate at post.*

10. The State Department must work with Congress to restore the Capital Security Cost Sharing Program [for embassy construction] at its full capacity, adjusted for inflation to approximately $2.2 billion in fiscal year 2015.

- *The FY14 President's Budget included a request for $2.2 billion in the Embassy Security, Construction, and Maintenance account.*

11. The Board supports the State Department's initiative to request additional Marines and expand the Marine Security Guard (MSG) Program – as well as corresponding requirements for staffing and funding.

- *Along with the Congress and Department of Defense, we are working to increase the number of Marine Security Guards at U.S. diplomatic facilities, and have requested (and received) more resources to build facilities at additional posts to host Marine Security Guards in the future.*

STAFFING HIGH RISK, HIGH THREAT POSTS

12. The Board strongly endorses the Department's request for increased DS personnel for high- and critical-threat posts and for additional Mobile Security Deployment teams, as well as an increase in DS domestic staffing in support of such action.

- *With Congressional support, the Department is creating 151 new Diplomatic Security positions -- 113 are expected to be hired this fiscal year. The remainder will be hired in FY14.*

13. The Department should assign key policy, program, and security personnel at high risk, high threat posts for a minimum of one year. For less critical personnel, the temporary duty length (TDY) length should be no less than 120 days.

- *All high threat posts now have a minimum of a one-year tour of duty. We are planning to ensure overlap between incumbent and incoming positions to facilitate continuity of operations at high threat posts.*
- *Temporary duty assignments are set at a minimum of 120 days.*

14. The Department needs to review the staffing footprints at high risk, high threat posts, with particular attention to ensuring adequate Locally Employed Staff (LES) and management support. High risk, high threat posts must be funded and the human resources process prioritized to hire LES interpreters and translators.

- *The Department surveyed every post to review the numbers of interpreters and translators on staff, and found that there was adequate staffing.*

15. With increased and more complex diplomatic activities in the Middle East, the Department should enhance its ongoing efforts to significantly upgrade its language capacity, especially Arabic, among American employees, including DS, and receive greater resources to do so.

- *The Department is ramping up the language capacity of its American employees, including Diplomatic Security agents, especially in Arabic. Increasing language capacity takes time – certain languages take up to 2 years to learn. In the short term, the Department is committed to better equipping the growing cadre of security experts to engage local populations and cooperate with host nation security forces.*

TRAINING AND AWARENESS

16. A panel of Senior Special Agents and Supervisory Special Agents should revisit DS high-threat training with respect to active internal defense and fire survival as well as Chief of Mission protective detail training.

- *The Department established a panel of Supervisory Special Agents to participate in a Program Review of the High Threat Tactical Course; as a result, DS revised high-threat training and COM protective detail training and raised standards for passing the High Threat Tactical Course. DS and the Foreign Service Institute are currently revising the curriculum.*
- *DS is pursuing a high-threat training strategy that will incorporate elements of this training across the full spectrum of courses required for DS special agents throughout their careers.*

17. The Diplomatic Security Training Center and Foreign Service Institute should collaborate in designing joint courses that integrate high threat training and risk management decision processes for senior and mid-level DS agents and Foreign Service Officers and better prepare them for leadership positions in high risk, high threat posts.

- *The Department has enhanced security training efforts, including by requiring personnel headed to high threat posts to receive additional, specialized security training.*

SECURITY AND FIRE SAFETY EQUIPMENT

18. The Department should ensure provision of adequate fire safety and security equipment for safe havens and safe areas in non-Inman/SECCA facilities, as well as high threat Inman facilities.

- *The Department has surveyed fire and life safety equipment requirements abroad and is now upgrading this equipment, to include enhanced fire safety equipment and personal protective equipment, at all high-threat, high-risk U.S. diplomatic posts abroad.*

19. There have been technological advancements in non-lethal deterrents, and the State Department should ensure it rapidly and routinely identifies and procures additional options for non-lethal deterrents in high risk, high threat posts and trains personnel on their use.

- *The Department has addressed this recommendation.*

20. DS should upgrade surveillance cameras at high risk, high threat posts for greater resolution, nighttime visibility, and monitoring capability beyond post.

- *Over the next year the Department will have upgraded high-threat, high-risk facilities with more modern surveillance cameras that feature greater resolution and monitoring capability at all times of day.*

INTELLIGENCE AND THREAT ANALYSIS

21. Careful attention should be given to factors showing a deteriorating threat situation in general as a basis for improving security posture. Key trends must be quickly identified and used to sharpen risk calculations.

- *The Department has addressed this recommendation.*

22. The DS Office of Intelligence and Threat Analysis should report directly to the DS Assistant Secretary and directly supply threat analysis to all DS components, regional Assistant Secretaries, and Chiefs of Mission in order to get key security-related threat information into the right hands more rapidly.

- *The DS Office of Intelligence and Threat Analysis, now reports directly to the Assistant Secretary for Diplomatic Security for threat reporting and supplies threat analysis to regional Assistant Secretaries and Chiefs of Mission.*

PERSONNEL ACCOUNTABILITY

23. The Board is of the view that findings of unsatisfactory leadership performance by senior officials in relation to the security incident under review should be a potential basis for discipline recommendations by future ARBs, and would recommend a revision of Department regulations or amendment to the relevant statute to this end.

- *The Department is working with Congress to increase accountability. In January, the Department proposed legislation to grant future ARBs the authority to recommend disciplinary action on the basis of unsatisfactory leadership, and thus increase accountability for security incidents.*

24. The Board was humbled by the courage and integrity shown by those on the ground in Benghazi and Tripoli, in particular the DS agents and Annex team who defended their colleagues… We trust that the Department and relevant agencies will take the opportunity to recognize their exceptional valor and performance, which epitomized the highest ideals of government service.

- *The President and the Secretary of State have publicly mentioned the bravery and heroic efforts of our personnel on numerous occasions.*

The Department bestowed the Holbrooke award on Ambassador Chris Stevens; the Thomas Jefferson award to the personnel who gave their lives in September; the Secretary's award to one officer who was seriously injured; and the Secretary's Heroism Award to 12 personnel who defended the Benghazi facilities.